NINA SADUR

The Witching Hour and Other Plays

Edited
by NADYA L. PETERSON

BOSTON
2 0 1 4

Copyright © 2014 Academic Studies Press
All rights reserved

ISBN 978-1-61811-398-6 (hardback)
ISBN 978-1-61811-399-3 (paperback)
ISBN 978-1-61811-400-6 (electronic)

Book design by Ivan Grave
On the cover: Nina Sadur's portrait by Mikhail Kopyov,
   reproduced by the artist's permission.

Published by Academic Studies Press in 2014
28 Montfern Avenue
Brighton, MA 02135, USA
press@academicstudiespress.com
www.academicstudiespress.com

Contents

Acknowledgments

~ *4* ~

Introduction. Nina Sadur's Fantastic Theater,
by Mark Lipovetsky
translated by Nadya L. Peterson

~ *6* ~

Go!
translated by Nadya L. Peterson

~ *14* ~

Pechorin: In Memoriam
translated by Margarit T. Ordukhanyan

~ *49* ~

Red Paradise
translated by Nadya L. Peterson
and Kathryn Szczepanska

~ *115* ~

The Witching Hour
translated by Anna Gordeychuk
and Nadya L. Peterson

~ *153* ~

Afterword, *by Karin Sarsenov*

~ *192* ~

List of References

~ *202* ~

Acknowledgments

I have wanted to bring Nina Sadur's brilliant plays to the English-speaking public since I first read them in the 1990s. My first thanks, therefore, go to Nina Sadur, whose plays inspire, fascinate, and awe her readers and whose generous decision to entrust her work to me is greatly appreciated.

The challenge of translating and interpreting Sadur's drama for this volume could not have been met without the participation of a number of dedicated translators, editors, and critics. This was a truly collaborative effort that drew most of its support from the Hunter College community.

Some of the translators, such as Margarit Ordukhanyan, Kathryn Szczepanska, and myself, teach at Hunter. Anna Gordeychuk, another translator for the volume, graduated from Hunter and started her work on Sadur when a student in my course on translation. Emma Eklof, whose acumen and discernment in all matters related to language and writing was of tremendous help in the initial phase of the work, also studied at Hunter. Betsy Hulick, a prominent translator of Russian literature, is an important presence and frequent participant at Hunter's cultural events. Betsy's editorial insights and suggestions were invaluable in the final stages of the project. Finally, the publication of the volume was generously supported by the Hunter College Filia Holtzman Fund.

The task of interpreting Sadur's drama in its historical and literary context fell to two outstanding experts on Soviet and post-Soviet literature, Karin Sarsenov and Mark Lipovetsky. I want to thank both of them for their unhesitating decision to join the project and for their significant contributions to this volume.

I also want to thank Bill Glass for generously agreeing to listen to read-throughs of the plays and for providing his writerly point of view on Sadur's language and dialog. Finally, I want to express my profound gratitude to Sharona Vedol, the editor responsible for preparing the volume for the Academic Studies Press, for her expertise and interest in the project.

Introduction

Nina Sadur's Fantastic Theater

Mark Lipovetsky

The theater of Nina Sadur is like a baroque curiosity chamber inhabited by all kinds of monstrosities— a young, tender, black-eyed vampire witch, werewolves that kill out of compassion, aliens, and even talking hair. All are presented against the backdrop of daily life with easily recognizable characters: vocational school students, bored ladies and their wealthy husbands, homeless bums and alcoholics, ex-cons and unmarried train engineers. The distinction between fantasy and realism (or naturalism, to be more precise) is neither essential nor discernible. Reality is fantastic, and the world of monsters familiar and lived-in. Sadur builds her dramatic action in a way that makes her protagonists, as well as her readers and spectators, incapable of differentiating between reality and fantasy or delusion; the majority of her plays are akin to mysteries that lack final resolutions. Even when a solution is offered, in the end ambivalence about what is real and what is fantastic is always inevitably and immediately reinstated.

Sadur's theater emerged in the early 1980s from a curious mélange of influences that shaped the literary underground of the late Soviet period. On the one hand, her work in the theater is clearly inspired by the culture of decadence, primarily symbolist drama, represented by works ranging from Maurice Maeterlinck's plays and Oscar Wilde's *Salomé* to the dramatic works of Alexander Blok, Leonid Andreev, and Nikolai Evreinov. On the other hand, in Sadur's work the metaphysical and philosophical background associated with decadence is infused with contemporary reality and populated by contemporary characters, all viewed through the prism of the theater of the absurd (Becket and Ionesco, first published in the Soviet Union in the 1960s, were widely read at the time). Together, this paradoxical combination of influences generates an effect closely reminiscent of Jean Baudrillard's "hyperreality of simulacra." Although the eminent French philosopher was developing his ideas on the issue at about the same time as Sadur was writing her best plays, neither his name nor his concepts became known in Russia until much later. Similarities between perceptions of Soviet society current in the literary underground of the time (as, for example, in Andrei Bitov's *Pushkin House*) and Baudrillard's analysis of late capitalism suggest that, despite its alleged isolation, Soviet society was experiencing evolutional and cultural crises analogous to those of its Western counterpart.

The Witching Hour (1983), a work included in this collection, offers the key to Sadur's phantasmagoric theater and artistic philosophy. In the first part of the play (*The Field*), an ordinary Soviet office worker, Lidya Petrovna, is sent with her colleagues to help with the potato harvest in the countryside. When Lidya gets lost amidst the endless empty fields, she meets a certain "Auntie." At first appearing either demented or clairvoyant or both, "Auntie" increasingly assumes the characteristics of a wood demon, deliberately leading Lidya astray and preventing her from finding her way back to safety. Equated with nature and death (her last name is Slayer), "Auntie" defines herself as "the evil of the world." Sadur does not, however, link nature to the "laws of eternity" or the higher meaning of life in this instance; nor does she set nature in opposition to the hollowness of social laws and interactions. Her "Auntie" is a sinister and dangerous she-demon; any contact with her causes extraordinary anxiety and heartache. Sadur's "Auntie" in fact embodies a mystical knowledge about the chaotic depths hidden beneath the surface of daily life.

The she-demon Slayer offers her fellow traveler a bizarre ritualistic challenge. Slayer will try to run away. Lidya will try to catch her. If Lidya succeeds, there will be heaven on earth. If not, the world will end. Lidya at first agrees to Slayer's conditions, but at the last moment becomes fearful of the she-demon's threats and falters. As a punishment for Lidya's defeat, the she-demon destroys the earth's upper layer and all who dwell there and convinces Lidya that she is left alone in the world and that her ordinary life is now only an imitation created by "Auntie" for Lidya's comfort.

In the second part of the play (*The Office*) Lidya Petrovna admits to her colleagues that since her meeting with the she-demon she has lost her certainty about the reality of the world around her ("I even doubt my own children, you know? Now, even they confuse me and trouble my heart.") When her boss, who is enamored of her, tries to kiss her, she reacts in an odd way: "A clone is trying to kiss me. A fake, an imitation. [...] You can't even fire me now because you don't exist!"

Remarkably, her coworkers believe Lidya's assertions without much hesitation. The mystical explanation offered by the she-demon fits with the private feelings of people trying to shield themselves with daily routines and preoccupations from eternal and unanswerable questions about the purpose of life. The major challenge for all characters in the play is to prove their existence. The sole possible solution offered is to escape the customary limits of life, "to jump out of oneself." But jump where? Lidya "jumps" into insanity. Lidya's answer to the challenge of proving her existence, essentially an escape into death, hardly suffices, however, to bring relief to Sadur's protagonist. Accompanied by the wailing of an ambulance, Lidya shouts: "Only my heart, my heart has stopped. I'm alone, but I lie in the deep, moist earth, and the world blooms, happy, joyous, and alive! Farewell! Live long and prosper, love, give birth, work and rest! Farewell!" The inability of any character in the play aside from the she-demon to find convincing proof of the authenticity of his or her own existence imparts a tragic irony to the idea of the "blooming of the world."

The connection of this dramatic parable to the notions of simulacra and simulation, which are central to the postmodernist philosophy of Jean Baudrillard, is indisputable. Sadur, however, amplifies this general philosophical orientation through use of the mystical grotesque. In Sadur's theater, a character ordinarily discovers the "simulativeness" of his, or more often her, environment directly after encountering chaos—death, insanity, and darkness. It is thanks not to social or cultural reasons, but purely metaphysical ones, that the familiar world loses its firm contours and turns into a fragile and terrifying illusion.

Virtually all of Sadur's characters are bewildered by the inauthenticity of the world and people around them. In "Comrades," the characters find proof of their own existence by fulfilling needs the other people have for them. But this solution to the riddle is shown to be fraught with danger, first because Sadur's heroes do not actually hear or see each other, focusing above all else on themselves and their everyday problems. Each character is locked in a cage of his or her own concerns. People are brought together only by dreams of happiness, shared illusions, or fears. Thus in the mini-play "Frozen" (1987), two cleaning ladies, Nadya and Leila, complain about loneliness and neglect but do not really communicate otherwise. The two women are connected solely by a fantastic reverie about a house on the seashore, children, a tender husband, and the shared vision of a terrifying, hellish god whose image emerges in puddles of dirty melted snow.

Second, when Sadur's characters do manage to "jump out of themselves" and bond with others, the connection, deeper than any found in "our ordinary clueless life," inevitably leads to tragic consequences. In Sadur, the veil of the daily grind conceals the universal chaos of existence. Any attempt to establish contact at this depth is doomed to catastrophic failure. The originality of Sadur's philosophical position lies in the writer's take on the incompatibility of human motivations. Her characters desperately try to shield themselves from chaos, while inexorably succumbing to its hypnotic and lethal call.

Sadur's "rewrites" of the classics of Russian literature are similarly grounded in her philosophy. At first glance, her *Pechorin: In Memoriam* (1999), an adaptation of Mikhail Lermontov's *A Hero of Our Time* which is included in this collection, faithfully follows the plot of the classical novel. Yet Sadur reconfigures the original work so that Pechorin, the novel's protagonist, gradually assumes the features of the "Russian Vampire," a living embodiment of chaos. Torn apart by despair, Sadur's Pechorin is nevertheless fatefully attractive to those around him. However, it is not his sexual prowess or intellect that appeal so much to his victims, but rather, the power of darkness he exudes but cannot control.

Sadur's play *Pannochka* (1985-86) similarly reworks Nikolai Gogol's "mystical thriller," *Vii*, another classical work of nineteenth century Russian literature. Characteristically, Sadur omits the mysterious pagan demon Vii in her adaptation. Instead, Gogol's protagonist, the vagabond seminary student Khoma Brut, is tested by the beauty of the young witch Pannochka. In the play, Sadur brilliantly recreates the Gogolian atmosphere of the opulent yet simple life of the Cossacks, with its heavy drinking, joyous gluttony, and voluptuous women. The seminarian is at home in this environment, delighted by its attractions. However, when submitting to the young witch (she saddles him like a horse, forcing him to fly her about), Khoma hears voices from a different and singularly beautiful world, a world that enchants him.

> What is it that rings, sings, splashes, and sucks the spirit out of my body? It's impossible for a good Christian to endure this sweetness. This bliss is a terror for the soul. Human eyes cannot bear seeing this—alive, churning in the mist.... Oh Lord, everything is alive ... frolicking ... and looking at you ... and calling you ... everything everywhere is laughing and kissing.... Your entire earth, oh Lord!

In Sadur, God is beauty, regardless of whether the source of this beauty is darkness or light. That is why, at the moment of Khoma's demise, the decrepit, defiled church collapses around him and Pannochka. Only the face of the Child, shining with an almost unbearable radiant light, rises above the ruins.

During each of the three funeral services Khoma has to conduct for Pannochka, killed by him in her witch's incarnation, he attempts to protect himself from the power of her beauty with prayer. But his proximity to the abyss turns out to be fatal. How can this power be overcome? After the first night, Khoma is revived by the carnal beauty of a young woman from the village. Thoughts about the stability of family life, home, and household bring a fleeting sense of peace. A rowdy fight with a Cossack after the second night restores Khoma's spirits, despite the fact that the Cossack is adversely affected by the event, becoming listless, sad, and gloomy afterward.

These shields, however, offer only a temporary protection against the call of the abyss, Khoma's love for Pannochka. It is because of this love that Khoma responds to her pitiful cries and, while fully aware of the disastrous consequences of the gesture, cannot but look at her after she "tenderly" asks him to do so. Khoma is willing to abandon his connection to earthly beauty and perish because of his inescapable attraction to chaos, the idea visually represented by the two protagonists' final embrace.

In Sadur's theater, this moment of unity in love is, essentially, the only possible resolution to the writer's philosophical dilemma. The everyday world is rejected in her plays as inauthentic and constrained. Yet, according to the logic of this theater, to venture beyond the limits of a reality based in simulacra is to enter the sphere of metaphysical darkness (chaos, death, and insanity), i.e. inexorable self-annihilation. Enchantment by beauty, born of chaos, often fatal or catastrophic in its consequences, is the sole viable proof of the reality of human existence, the only possible way for people to "jump out of themselves" and obtain freedom.

In this regard, Sadur's *The Red Paradise* (1988), also included in this collection, can be viewed as self-parody, but also undoubtedly as a response to the social concerns of the day. The plot of this absurdist mystical farce parodies numerous films and narratives concerning the search for eternal life, riches, and youth. Partaking of the eternal mysteries, however, does not guarantee depth of character. In the play, all participants are completely immersed in everyday life and are therefore lacking in that which comprises real life: love, pain, and freedom. It is precisely the simulative essence of their existence that is comically bared in the refrain, "No one dies here!" What at first appears to be the attainment of mystical knowledge turns out to be testimony to the characters' inauthenticity. They do not die because they do not live. For Sadur, the comic aspect of the core premise of the play borders on tragic. If it appeared before that an encounter with chaos, death, and void could reveal that which is authentic, then in *The Red Paradise* there is no such encounter at all. The hero experiencing death remains the same vulgar non-entity as before.

Sadur's disappointment with the social circumstances of the late 1980s and the 1990s is partially responsible for the writer's loss of faith. The slow revolution, unwittingly caused by perestroika, and the catastrophic decade after the collapse of the Soviet social system, were clearly presaged in Sadur's mystical theater. This was the encounter with chaos that she had anticipated, called for, and feared. Yet as early as 1988, well before the collapse of the Soviet regime and at the very peak of perestroika, Sadur appeared to understand that the anticipated upheaval was not destined to bring about a true revival—there was nothing left to revive. Late Soviet society was populated by full-fledged embodiments of "cynical reason," the term coined by Peter Sloterdijk in his assessment of the Enlightenment. If Communism is seen as the extreme case of an Enlightenment utopia, then Sloterdijk's "new cynicism" is the malady that afflicts Sadur's heroes:

> Enlightened false consciousness: this formulation should be regarded not as an incidental phrase but as a systematic approach, as a diagnostic model.... Disillusionment with enlightenment is by no means only a sign that epigones can and must be more critical than the founders. The characteristic odor of modern cynicism is of a more fundamental nature: a constitution of consciousness afflicted with enlightenment that, having learned from historical experience, refuses cheap optimism. New values? No, thanks! With the passing of defiant hopes, the listlessness of egoism pervades. In the new cynicism, a detached negativity comes through that scarcely allows itself any hope, at most a little irony and pity.[1]

---

[1] *Critique of Cynical Reason* (Minneapolis, MN: University of Minnesota Press, 1987), 6.

Thus, even if a metaphysical shock to the very core of being can disturb the process of simulation of values, it cannot jolt people out of their simulative existence. In other words, even a fundamental social catastrophe cannot reveal to the post-Soviet cynic, with his love of guaranteed comforts, the value and dangers of freedom. The first Putin decade was a confirmation of Sadur's vision. Perhaps that is why the beginning of the twenty-first century marked a long hiatus in Sadur's work as a playwright.

Sadur's drama has exerted a tremendous influence on contemporary Russian literature. Working essentially in isolation, she was able to combine early twentieth- century dramatic discourse with that of the late Soviet era. Having built a bridge between the two eras, Sadur paved the way for the rise of the new Russian drama of the 2000s, as evidenced in the work of the brothers Presniakov (*Terrorism*, *Playing the Victim*) Vasili Sigarev (*Wolfy*), Ivan Vyrypaev (*Euphoria*, *July*), and others. It was from Sadur that many of these playwrights learned to view a terrifying daily life as theater of the absurd against a backdrop of metaphysical chaos, and to see ritual immersion in the void as a possible (hoped-for) path toward regeneration, anticipating a new life and a new freedom.

Translated from the Russian
*by **Nadya L. Peterson***

GO!

A Play in One Act

CHARACTERS

AN ENGINE DRIVER

A PEASANT

AN OLD LADY IN BOOTS

Winter. Late night. Railroad tracks. A very remote place. Somewhere in the distance the lights of a small village twinkle in the snow. A peasant is kneeling on the tracks, preparing to die. He looks up at the sky, then lowers his head on the rail. The rumble of an approaching train is heard. One can't see the train, but the whorls of light and snow and the noise tell us that the train has passed on another track and signaled to the peasant. The peasant raises his head, looks after the train rushing past and puts his face on the rail again. The rail is cold.He tucks his hat under his cheek. Time passes. He hasn't moved. The train meets another in the distance. The driver who saw the peasant remarks to the other: "Hey Vit', some punk is down on the rail on the 500th kilometer." "It'll mess up the schedule, shit." "Brake, Vit', brake—the hell with the schedule!" These comments sound from far away where the train is now beginning to brake, but the peasant doesn't hear, he is still patiently lying there when the engine driver enters.

DRIVER   Like I said, that piece of shit is still here!

> *He comes up to the peasant and kicks him forcefully. The man falls*
> *on the rails, then meekly gets up and again arranges himself*
> *in the same pose: his face on the rail, his backside facing the stars.*
> *The driver kicks him again.*

This one is for messing up the schedule!

> *The peasant assumes the same pose. The driver kicks him.*

And this is for my bonus.

> *He remains as before. The driver kicks him.*

And this is for the investigation. (*Kicks him again.*) And this is for the stress. (*Kicks him again.*) And this one — for the stupid suicide attempt.

> *The peasant jumps up and hits the driver in the face.*
> *He falls down, and the peasant arranges himself on the rail again.*

DRIVER (*getting up*)   What are you, a lunatic? A lunatic, for sure. Why are you fighting me, you punk? I had to stop the train for you, mess up my schedule. Now God only knows what's gonna happen, and you hit me in the face?

PEASANT   Go ahead, mister.

DRIVER   Wow, the asshole can talk. Do you know how many crazies like you I've run over? Not one of them talked. Hey, you, get off the rail!

> *He pushes the peasant off the rail, starts to leave, but the peasant*
> *lies back down on the rail. A pause.*

Hey man, you want to die or what?

PEASANT   I wanna die.

DRIVER   I'll run you over.

PEASANT   Go ahead, do it.

DRIVER   Hey, hey, hey man, you ... you ... you....

PEASANT   Go on, mister.

DRIVER   All right, you listen now, creep, get off the rail.... No. 165 is right behind. It's a freight-train.

> *The peasant is silent.*

Why did I stop in the first place? I'm such an idiot, a stupid idiot…. I shouldn't have listened to Tolik. Would've been on my way by now, given my report, and started back again. (*Shouts.*) Time is passing, you know, it's passing! Time which belongs to the state, by the way; money is being wasted every second … what an idiot I am…. (*Looks around.*) I should tie you down, but there's nothing around, just snow. Come on, man, get up, let me pass!

PEASANT   No!

DRIVER   Yeeesss…. (*Sits on the rail nearby, lights a cigarette.*) We're definitely not moving. (*Listens.*) What's that? Wolves? Whining, just whining. Hey, listen, they won't come near us, will they?

PEASANT   No.

DRIVER   Or they might eat us up…. The air is good here, just like at a resort, not like in the city. Why don't you sit up now? Your face will freeze to the rail…. You see I haven't gone.

PEASANT   You'd better get moving.

DRIVER   "You'd better get moving." *You* try running a man over.

PEASANT (*sits up*)   Yeah, that's bad, it's true. (*Thinks.*) You should have a head start.

DRIVER   Sure. I am running now. Can't wait.

PEASANT   You're a sissy.

DRIVER   I'm not trying to pass for strong.

PEASANT   You weren't in the war.

DRIVER   No. I wasn't. I wish we'd never have it, anyhow. I hate war!

PEASANT   Think of me as the enemy. And — get moving.

Go! ∽

DRIVER   You *are* the enemy. Anyone who makes an attempt on his own life has no regard for other people.

The peasant hits the driver in the face.

(*Getting up.*) You're such a jerk. I've never seen such a stupid jerk. And now he's hitting me, the jerk.

PEASANT   You get going, mister!

DRIVER   And *you* stop hitting me.

PEASANT   And *you* get going!

DRIVER   And *you* don't tell *me* what to do! He hits you! He orders you around. Jumped out of nowhere. Crawled out from under a rock, like a bug. There's nothing but snow all around. And he lies down on the rail. How did Tolik see you in the first place?!

PEASANT (*gloomy*)   He has a sharp eye.

DRIVER   I don't understand why people don't want to live. You figure, if there's a war, we'll all go, anyway. Someone pushes the button—and it's fuck all! People should live just for now, it's good to live, isn't it? You have everything, why not live? But no, he doesn't feel like living. He lies down. Smack in the middle of the rail. And you have to run him over. Why not let the wolves eat you…. Yeah, right, why don't you just clear out, eh? They don't have a schedule … they'll eat you, why must you keep the train stalled?

PEASANT   A wolf is a wild animal.

DRIVER   Well, go join the wild animals since you don't want to live.

19

PEASANT   You wanna kick in the face?

DRIVER   Whoa, man. Or I'll kick *you*, even though you're an old man. So touchy! It should be all the same to you, you're looking to die.

PEASANT   You talk too much.

DRIVER   *I know* how much I should talk. And *you're* not telling me to stop. Now it's wild animals he doesn't like. But he shoves his stupid head in front of all those people on the train! And they're sitting there, innocently drinking tea. Fourteen cars. They look out the windows, and they don't see anything. They're worried because we've been stopped here for too long, God knows where, in some field … they complain to the conductor, they're bored. They have … children … they're going to see their relatives … friends … they're on vacation … they're living their lives, having dinner, making their beds, they want to get on with their trip … they drink tea. These are people, you understand? With tickets. Do you think all these people and me want to run you over? They're drinking tea, and I have to ruin their day?

PEASANT   You can tell them it's an accident.

DRIVER   Well! Lying is wrong, that's something we learned in school. And they have children, by the way! So I'll run over you with the children on board. It's nothing to you, but they'll carry it with them for the rest of their lives! They have to grow up, those children!

Pause.

PEASANT   I'm not going to the wild animals. Get on that train, mister, and do your job.

DRIVER   Oh, you lousy baaastard....

PEASANT   Your schedule's all screwed up.

DRIVER   Screwed up! And it'll go on being screwed up as long as you keep shoving your stupid shaved head....

PEASANT   My stupid head....

DRIVER   Yeah, shaved.

PEASANT   You're not the one who gave me a haircut.

DRIVER   Everybody knows where they do that.

PEASANT   Yeah, anywhere.

DRIVER   Well, my head isn't shaved, is it?

PEASANT   You better get going before it is.

DRIVER   Because of you, for sure. Or do you think they're just gonna pat me on the back for running you over?

PEASANT   You won't get a haircut just because of me.

DRIVER   Why not?

PEASANT   I'm all used up. Wasted.

DRIVER   Look at that, what a prince.

PEASANT   Well, maybe I *am* a prince.

DRIVER   I don't understand—why all this posturing? Why don't you just go and hang yourself like everyone else if you don't like the wild animals. You've chosen a selfish way to do it, I'll say that.

PEASANT   I kinda thought about it....

DRIVER   And?

PEASANT   It's scary somehow....

DRIVER   Whaaat? (*Roars with laughter.*) Wow, what a comedian! Do you know what you'll look like after the "accident"? You'll look like minced meat!

PEASANT   I don't want to hang in a noose.

DRIVER   Just like a prince, shit! (*After a pause.*) I don't know. I'm alive, right?

PEASANT (*darkly*)   So?

DRIVER   Don't you "so" me.... I'm a bachelor, by the way, but never mind that. Man, you could be my father. And this is my life ... I live alone, fool that I am!

PEASANT   How come?

DRIVER   Well, it's just that I don't know how to hustle. Everybody hustles nowadays. But I don't want to, you know. I have a conscience.

PEASANT   So what?

DRIVER   It's something else that's been eating at me. I live on my paycheck, right? You know, we're paid well.... But some of us think it's not enough. I used to have a partner, Golikov, he stole twenty-eight whistles.

PEASANT   So what?

DRIVER   No, it's not that. A train whistle, you know how much it's worth? Seventy rubles. And he—he got twenty-eight of them. They broke open his locker, they just thought it was suspicious all those whistles disappearing. Who wants a life like that anyway? His wife's just like him. They're both dressed

Go! ∽

to the nines. She has gold up to here (*gestures*), even in her teeth. And she works at a chocolate factory. Once Golikov gave me a chocolate and told me they were like eighty-five rubles a kilo. The wife steals some and then eats them outside. He gave me half a chocolate to taste....

PEASANT   So what?

DRIVER   Tell me, please, did you do that in the war?

PEASANT   What do you want me to say?

DRIVER   Would you give a comrade half a candy? Half?! Even though they sell for eighty-five a kilo?

PEASANT   But he got caught.

DRIVER   Who?

PEASANT   The candy man.

DRIVER   Yeah, he got caught.

PEASANT   So?

DRIVER   No, I don't want to live like that.

PEASANT   So what?

DRIVER   I just don't understand it, is it that he's not afraid, or doesn't he give a damn?

PEASANT   Who?

DRIVER   That partner of mine, Golikov.

PEASANT   But he got caught.

DRIVER   True, they didn't have any kids. But suppose she had a baby and wanted to breastfeed it, with her shining gold teeth.

PEASANT   Are you crazy, or what?

DRIVER   Why?

PEASANT   Why keep talking about them?

DRIVER   It's just that I don't want to hustle.

PEASANT   So don't.

A pause.

It's cold.

DRIVER   You're past caring, so I'll tell you everything. I haven't told this to anyone, by the way. But you're ... well, you don't have much time left, so I'll tell you.

PEASANT   So what is it now?

DRIVER   I don't know how to get a girl.

PEASANT   Not even once?

DRIVER   Get off it! No, I mean like getting married. We'll get married and then she'll have a baby, and she'll make me hustle.

PEASANT   So you'll hustle.

DRIVER   I have a conscience. The kid'll grow up and, no matter how hard I'll try to hide it, it'll come out.

PEASANT   What'll come out?

DRIVER   That his parents were hustlers!

PEASANT   Have you finished now, or what?

DRIVER   What?

PEASANT   The schedule!

DRIVER   Shit, and here I am, standing around like an idiot.... I should get going, well, you see ... and you were saying ... well. Good-bye.

PEASANT   Good-bye.

The driver leaves. The peasant lies down on the rails.

DRIVER   You! You!

PEASANT   Get going, mister!

A pause.

DRIVER   What are you doing? I shared with you, you prick, I told you … my whole entire life!

PEASANT   It's cold. Get going, mister.

DRIVER   So you've got a conscience or not? I'm thirty-two years old! I've got my whole life ahead of me! My Mom's still around! I'm an honest man! I haven't spilled anybody's blood! When I visit my Mom I can't even kill the chickens! Why do you keep at me?! What have I done? I opened my heart to you. And you keep doing this!

PEASANT (*gets up*)   Dirt.

Pause.

DRIVER   And who are you, anyhow?

PEASANT   I'm nobody. And you're dirt.

DRIVER   What can you do with a psycho? Get out of here! Or I'll call for help and get someone to tie you up.

PEASANT   Look up there…. (*Points to the sky.*)

DRIVER   Look yourself. (*Spits.*) Idiot.

PEASANT   You were talking away just now but nobody was listening up there. Dirt! Zero.

DRIVER   Are you a Baptist or what? Fucking Baptist. No use talking to a Baptist. I'm gonna go get help.

PEASANT   I'll hide. Your train will leave, and I'll lie down again. It's better to have this out now. Get going, mister.

DRIVER   There's nothing I can do?

PEASANT   Looks like it.

DRIVER   You're set on this?

PEASANT   I am.

DRIVER   And nothing in the world interests you anymore?

PEASANT   Nothing.

DRIVER (*yells*)   I'm freezing! We'll all freeze!

PEASANT   Move around some. Warm yourself.

DRIVER   All right. I am relieving myself of any responsibility. I'm going for help, let the next driver decide, my shift's almost over, and my partner's about to replace me…. (*Starts to leave.*)

The peasant whistles, calling him.

DRIVER   Now what?

*The peasant's attitude suddenly changes. He is now an "ex-con"
with an attitude.*

PEASANT   How come you don't ask?

DRIVER (*taken aback a bit*)   Ask what?

PEASANT (*nods toward the rails*)   You know…. That…. Aren't you interested?

DRIVER (*as if not understanding*)   Interested in what?

PEASANT   I want to end it, and you don't even ask why.

DRIVER   It's clear. You've been under a great deal of stress.

PEASANT   Stress?

DRIVER   When a man is dealt some great blow and it's too much for him, the result is stress.

PEASANT   Some great blow, you say….

Go! ∽

DRIVER   There are specialists who deal with this sort of thing.

PEASANT   Yeah, I got dealt … all right….

DRIVER   There are doctors who specialize in this kind of condition. Educated. Experienced.

PEASANT   Something really hit me….

DRIVER   Listen! You called me dirt, and I let it go. Just listen to me, there are experts who know this stuff, they'll be able to ….help you … that's their job…. Come on, come with me!

PEASANT   You know what hit me?

DRIVER   Come on. I'll take you along. Let's get going! Stress is treatable … they have new methods, kindness, for example….

PEASANT   Nah. I'll tell you myself.

DRIVER   You need to go to the hospital! On my train! There are people there, tea, warmth, light! I'm offering you this myself! You'll get in treatment, they'll cure you with music.

PEASANT   You're the only one I'm going to tell.

DRIVER   I forgave you for calling me "dirt!"

PEASANT   You can't treat my kind of stuff with music. You can't think….

DRIVER (*interrupting*)   I'm telling you. Let's go, I won't give you away, I have a good partner, his name is Sania, you won't be alone….

PEASANT   I'm telling you, my….

DRIVER   My mother is old! She wants grandkids! And everybody's driving me crazy! She wants a grandson to dig in her vegetable garden with his little spade…. I don't need to put up with this shit! I'm not trying to be a hero! They have specialists, doctors. Let the passengers move on! Let them drink tea, let them even ... hustle ... if they're stupid enough.... I am just sorry for the kids, I don't want to hear about this!

PEASANT   What happened was, I go there and I say to her: "I got a headache for some reason...."

DRIVER   They have specialists, they'll know what to do.

PEASANT   I say to her, give me five rubles to buy wine, but she didn't give me any....

DRIVER   Oh, dear God....

PEASANT   She wouldn't....

DRIVER   Oh you ... and you....

The peasant spits.

They'll shoot you for that.

PEASANT   Who?

DRIVER   You.

PEASANT   Why?

DRIVER   For murder.

PEASANT   Whose murder?

DRIVER   Didn't you kill her?

PEASANT   No!

DRIVER   So what's the reason for all the stress?

PEASANT   You know, she wouldn't give me five rubles! For red wine!

Pause.

DRIVER   So that's why you…. (*Nods to the rails.*)

PEASANT   But she wouldn't….

The driver falls to his knees.

DRIVER   Hey….

PEASANT   What?

DRIVER   Tell me you're lying….

PEASANT   Go ask her yourself. The fat bitch, she sits there and says: "I won't give it to you, I need it for myself."

DRIVER   Tell me you're lying….

PEASANT   You're like a broken record, eh?

DRIVER   Listen, man, you don't go to your death for five rubles.

PEASANT   For the first time in a thousand years someone wants to do it, and he's not allowed to die in peace.

DRIVER   It's just five rubles. And life….

PEASANT   And I want my wine!!

Pause.

Get up, you'll freeze your legs off … then you'll walk (*walks on half-bended knees*) like a monkey.

DRIVER (*gets up, dusts himself off*)   So here's for you…. (*Searches his pockets.*)

PEASANT   I want my wine, you see, like a man, we're all people….

DRIVER (*nods*)   Sure…. (*Gives him the money.*) Here. Five rubles.

The peasant takes the money.

PEASANT (*slaps Driver on the shoulder*)   Great! A million thanks, pal.

DRIVER   You're welcome….

PEASANT   Say hello to your bosses! You can get moving now! Green light to you!

DRIVER   Wait! I'm telling you, wait! (*Stops the peasant.*) My mother is old!

PEASANT   And I'm an orphan.

DRIVER   You're lying, lying, lying! You're no orphan! You've killed! You're a murderer! You've killed, mutilated, and dismembered the body ... a cold-blooded murder with aggravating....

PEASANT (*fearfully*)   Cross yourself....

DRIVER   And what did you do time for? (*Snatches the hat from him.*) A shaved head. What did you do time for? Killing a man is like swatting a fly for you! So you killed again and got scared and put yourself on the rails! For five rubles!

PEASANT   Why do you keep at it?... I have the money now, you gave it to me yourself.... I'm leaving....

DRIVER   What did you do time for?

PEASANT   Ah,... I got drunk.

DRIVER   So ... you got drunk ... drunk ... there was a fight. You got out of jail ... people shunned you ... a criminal ... and you couldn't adapt!

PEASANT   I did.

DRIVER   You didn't! People spat on you because you're a criminal. I see how you'd want to die after that.

PEASANT   People accepted me like I was one of them. People aren't beasts, they don't spit on someone who's been punished already. (*Playing.*) But what's it to me? I left the camp, put on everything new. Bathed, wore a new jacket, a quilted jacket without a number, new underpants, a T-shirt. And a new cap. I knew where I was going—into the world. I had everything new on. And people said to me: Congratulations on your arrival, mister. Make yourself at home. Especially since you can drive a bulldozer.

DRIVER   What?

PEASANT   "Especially since you can drive a bulldozer." I drive a bulldozer!

DRIVER   You do?

PEASANT   Who else? *You*? You're a … shitty engine driver. Keeping the train stalled like that.

DRIVER   You … you … you must've busted the bulldozer and….

PEASANT   … put myself down on the rail? (*Gives him the finger.*) I'd never mess up a bulldozer! Get that straight!

DRIVER   So how did you end up on the rail?

PEASANT   You don't get it, do you?… Hey, why don't we—since we're stopped anyway and have five rubles—why don't we get some wine from Dus'ka? That's my village over there, see the lights shining?

DRIVER   I do. (*Looks up at the sky.*) Up there the stars are shining too.

PEASANT   They shine, but not for your kind! And there are people over there, let's get warm.

DRIVER   He came all this way to kill himself for five rubles.

PEASANT   It's all right. We've talked about it already…. Let's go, and…. I'm sick and tired of it all.

DRIVER (*sits down on the rails*) My brain aches. That's it. I'm screwed. (*Wistfully.*) I don't believe you. You're lying. You're angry. Angry. And evil.

PEASANT Who's angry? Let's go drink wine at Dus'ka's. And that fat ass can go fuck herself. She's the one who's angry.

DRIVER Bitch....

PEASANT Bitch. She has metal caps on her teeth. She bought herself new earrings. All she does is sit around.

DRIVER Bitch! She cheated!! On you!

PEASANT Maybe a hundred times! The man goes in to do time, a woman goes out to play. It's a law of nature.

DRIVER So how can one live?

PEASANT What do you mean?

DRIVER If everybody started throwing themselves under a train for five rubles, there'd be no need for war.

PEASANT And who needs war anyway? It's filthy all through.

DRIVER Hey, man. You fought in the war! You're part of the older generation, we owe you respect! You were willing to sacrifice your life for your country, for us.

PEASANT (*assuming a dignified air*) Well, that's true!

DRIVER And then, after that ... such a life ... such a heroic life ... you throw yourself on the rails for a lousy fiver! The young Communist pioneers look at you for guidance, you son of a bitch! And you throw yourself away! You're a traitor! You've betrayed us! You're betraying our generation! (*Hits the peasant in the face.*)

PEASANT (*getting up*) Don't you hit me, you little punk! Betray, betray! You cluck like a chicken! I haven't betrayed anyone yet! You're the one who betrayed your train! Asshole! Standing here like a stubborn bull. The governement entrusted you with a train, but you're stuck here. Me personally, I'm off to Dus'ka's. See you later, sucker.

DRIVER (*with feeling*) Hey, listen....

PEASANT So how come you're talking to a traitor?

DRIVER Life is good, eh?

PEASANT You don't say!!

DRIVER And I say, life is good, eh?

PEASANT So what's this all of a sudden?

DRIVER Simple! Life is good! (*Shakes the peasant.*) Life is good! Life is good! Life is good! Do you feel it?

PEASANT I sure do. But they should send *you* to the hospital. Let them treat *your* stress with music.

DRIVER Man, life is good.

PEASANT So live.

DRIVER We must!

PEASANT Aha.

DRIVER Life is more precious than anything.

PEASANT It depends.

DRIVER People have always struggled.

PEASANT True.

DRIVER The entire history of civilization rests on this. Beginning with the monkey.

PEASANT   The monkey is another story…. (*Spits.*) And a man is
another story.

DRIVER   Follow my thought. A man struggles—why?

PEASANT   Go ask him.

DRIVER   I'm asking you.

PEASANT   I've got what I wanted. (*Waves the bank note around.*)

DRIVER   Listen to me! A man struggles because he only has one
life, and that's it…. (*Looks around.*) See, there's nothing around
here. Just the elements. My partner started stealing whistles
to get more out of life, to distance himself from these … shitty
elements. To feel every little moment of life. Here he is, sitting—
click—and the color TV is on. Then he sits a while longer—
click!—his Japanese stereo's on. Then he sits longer still—click!—
and takes his car out for a drive. Every minute is filled with
luxury and comforts, so as not to … not to feel death. At night
he would turn his standing lamp on—with chimes. Shadows
make patterns on the walls, the bells are tinkling … and you
don't see the night! People try to fill their lives completely. If
you have talent, or if you're some kind of an artist, it doesn't
matter, all you need is your intense creativity. Or let's say you're
a scientist, then you just move the science along and don't care
about anything else. But if you're an ordinary man, then life is
more frightening, you need more than other people, you need
good food, you need comforts, children, and you need wads of
money! Do you see?

PEASANT   I do.

Go! ⤴

DRIVER   And what do *you* want?

PEASANT   But … you gave me what I want … money for red wine….

DRIVER   You're not a man. You're not a person. You are nothing.

Enter an old woman in boots.

OLD WOMAN   Hello, citizens!

DRIVER   Now what?

OLD WOMAN   You haven't seen my little goat, have you?

DRIVER   A little goat is all we need.

OLD WOMAN   But you see, he ran away! It's cold…. And he's running around outside.

Pause.

DRIVER   Granny, say … you … you've come all the way from the village, eh?

OLD WOMAN   From the village, citizens.

ENGINNER   Came all the way across the fields, did you? And you're looking for a goat in the middle of the night?

OLD WOMAN   But it's just that … you see, he's run away.

DRIVER (*looks at both of them*)   So is everybody like you in your village?

OLD WOMAN   Oh, we've got all kinds. People are busy, some watch movies, some just sit around….

DRIVER (*about the Peasant*)   But this one has a bee in his bonnet? Why is he so worked up?

OLD WOMAN   Well … you know, he's alive. All kinds of things can happen to a man.

35

ENIGNEER   No, you tell me, why does he wander around? You've
got to know, he's one of your kind.

Old Woman is puzzled.

OLD WOMAN   I think, maybe something set that little goat off.
He's not himself and he's getting old.

DRIVER   And I ask you, is this man from your village?!

OLD WOMAN   But I thought he was with you.

Pause.

I see the train broke down. I figure you're fixin' it. (*To the peasant.*)
You haven't seen my little goat, eh?

PEASANT   Nope.

DRIVER (*to Peasant*)   So you say you're from that village and you
got a woman. And have different kinds of animals … chickens
… a vegetable garden. What's the size of your potato field? Eh?
Why don't you answer me?

PEASANT   What's it to you?

DRIVER   How big is your potato field? My mother has one. I stop
by to help so she has her own spuds in the winter, turn the soil
over with my own hands. I'm a working man, I do everything
myself. But you…. (*To Granny.*) He doesn't have anything! He
doesn't even have a house! He lies about everything! He's lying
that he's from your village. Lowlife.

OLD WOMAN   I think … that … his face is somehow familiar.

DRIVER   Don't you lie too, granny. Old as you are! You could be
my mother, and still you lie. My mother's your age.

OLD WOMAN   I remember his face from somewhere....

DRIVER   False testimony can lead to punishment, you should know that.

OLD WOMAN   I think I remember his face.

PEASANT   I'm not one of your people, Granny. (*To Driver.*) Calm down now, I'm not. I don't belong with anybody. (*After a pause.*) I lay down on the rails … because of that....

DRIVER (*yelping*)   Not for five rubles, then! Are you trying to mess with my head, hobo?

PEASANT   I won't do it again. You can get going.

OLD WOMAN   I know this face.

DRIVER   I've always respected old ladies! They remind me of my mother! They've seen a lot, they've suffered! And by doing this, by siding with this filthy tramp, you humiliate yourself, you lose your self-respect. He's a homeless bum, useless.

OLD WOMAN   But citizens, what's all the fuss about? I'm sorry, of course, that everything's happening at once. My barn's falling in, so I put the little goat in the hallway for now. My chicken spends the winter there too, it's warm inside. And the goat, he's a fierce little thing, you know, he stops people from coming in. And he doesn't want to go back to the barn either. All right, if you don't want to go back, stay. But he won't let anybody in— when the Klykovs come, say, or the Tapkins, won't let them in my house. And, the funniest thing is, he doesn't do it because he's mean-tempered. He thinks he's protecting me…. From the Klykovs…. (*Laughs like a little girl.*)

DRIVER   What century are you from, lady?

OLD WOMAN   Well, you know … from this century.

DRIVER   What's all this about a goat then?

OLD WOMAN   Well, you know … he ran away … it's dark … and cold…. What should I do now? He probably … thought….

DRIVER   A goat cannot think.

OLD WOMAN   And how do you know that? Did he tell you what he thinks and what he doesn't?

DRIVER   And this from an old lady!

GRANNY (*to the Peasant*)   So they say to me—you should get rid of him.

PEASANT   And what business is it of theirs?

OLD WOMAN   The Klykovs. And even the Tapkins. All of them. And so he got mad and took off.

PEASANT   I can see that….

DRIVER   Now he's going to say something smart. Just listen to him.

PEASANT   The goat … he will … come back….

DRIVER   Ha-ha-ha!

OLD WOMAN   It's true! I think he will!

PEASANT   I've got a brother living in the village….

DRIVER   Aha, aha, just listen to him spinning tales. And maybe your Mom's still alive?

PEASANT   I'm an orphan.

DRIVER   He doesn't have a brother! He doesn't have anything!

PEASANT   He lives in the village, like you. He knows about animals.

OLD WOMAN   I believe him.

PEASANT   If you treat the little goat well, he'll … understand….

OLD WOMAN   Treat him well! I'll keep him in the entryway then.

PEASANT   That's the main thing … he'll understand….

OLD WOMAN   He'll understand!   He'll understand! (*To the Driver.*) He'll understand!

PEASANT   You don't keep him for the meat, but for your soul.

OLD WOMAN   Oh, thank you!

PEASANT   Don't give it another thought. The goat will come back.

OLD WOMAN   Thank you, thank you. How can I find anything here by myself?

PEASANT   I could take a look for you … if you like!

DRIVER   Good God! Look at that! And now who's gonna die?

PEASANT   You will.

DRIVER   He's just a hobo, lady, he wanders around homeless, useless … he has nothing to do.

OLD WOMAN   But who would wander around with nothing to do?…

DRIVER   He does! He's envious of people who ride the train, he doesn't like it that the cars are shiny … it's warm and light inside, and tea is served … they're traveling, and their little kids snooze like kittens, people all together … smoking a bit on the platform … the café car is beautiful … so that's why he wanders around!

PEASANT   All lies!

DRIVER   He wanders around! People ride the train, and then they can't—because he wanders!

PEASANT   Lies, total lies!

DRIVER   He wanders around, lady, he does!

OLD WOMAN   But there've always been wanderers. In olden times people wandered … when we had landowners. They always wandered.

DRIVER   You can't compare now to then. Those people were oppressed.

OLD WOMAN   Not oppressed at all. They just wandered and wandered. They would drink some milk, take some bread….

DRIVER   So they were hobos, too.

OLD WOMAN   No, not hobos at all. People wandered, looked at the world. The world is beautiful, you know.

DRIVER   What was so beautiful about it—a landowner?

OLD WOMAN   You think they looked at the landowner? They looked at the world. And then they kicked the landowner out. And people always wandered … in that war they did, and afterwards too, and when the Germans came—again they wandered … or when the world is sick a little—they start wandering, or they wander simply to see that the world is still standing … and they'll always wander to keep the world standing forever.

DRIVER   Your head is muddled from old age! You just lumped everybody together—hobos and … everybody else….

OLD WOMAN   Not at all. For the world to stand, one has to walk the earth. Everybody knows that. The world likes it when a man walks it by himself, doesn't fly over it in a rocket. What can you see from a rocket? You can forget yourself in that rocket. But here, right away, you can see what needs to be fixed, fed, cured. It depends … it's always been like that … people wander … so the earth doesn't get sick … that's why they wander … I'm saying this is why I know your face….

PEASANT   Mother … me too…. I … I think the same….

DRIVER   I can't believe him! *Moooo-theeer!!*

OLD WOMAN   Oh!

DRIVER   You say, walking the world, yes?

OLD WOMAN   Yes….

DRIVER   For it to bloom, for example, is that so?

OLD WOMAN   Well, yes.

PEASANT   And I … mother … mother … listen…. I feel there's something wrong! Something's wrong! Oh, my God!!!

DRIVER   But he did time! He's a criminal!

Pause.

PEASANT   I did time, mother.

OLD WOMAN (*to Driver*)   So why are *you* jumping around? Excuse me, but it's not you who did time. All sorts of things can happen to people. They aren't dead, you know. They can go astray. It's always been like that. They might not fit in with the rest and would go astray. So many people have done time, that's no reason … now … to throw yourself under a train.

DRIVER   Ah! But he did! Threw himself under!

Silence.

OLD WOMAN   But it would hurt....

DRIVER   But he doesn't give a damn! He doesn't care about his crushed bones, he just wants to ruin it for us! Look at me, kind people, here I am, lying in my own blood. He doesn't give a damn about anybody else. Can you imagine? I could ... shoot such people....

OLD WOMAN   You're so young! You say things without thinking! It hurts to live, you know....

DRIVER   But you were just saying! Well, I don't know, lady! The world is at peace ... birds are singing.... (*Points to the Peasant.*) And what is this? He's destroying himself. He dreams about killing himself.

OLD WOMAN   But the world wouldn't let him go. So I'm right then.

DRIVER   I'm the one who wouldn't let him go!

OLD WOMAN   So you're the one who's right then. Why are you so upset about it?

DRIVER   I don't give a damn. I don't need gratitude. I just want to know if anybody at all, some kind of vermin, especially a criminal, can just decide to stop a train....

OLD WOMAN   Well, we *are* standing here now.

DRIVER   No, but can an old, you know, hobo.... I bet he doesn't even have a passport.

PEASANT   I do!

OLD WOMAN   So what! The main thing is to be a man. What's so important about a passport?

Go!

DRIVER   The nerve!

PEASANT   Mother, I'll find your goat!

OLD WOMAN   Oh, thank you, dear citizen, many thanks!

DRIVER   Come off it! Don't you understand?

OLD WOMAN   What's this again?

DRIVER   He needs a roof over his head!

PEASANT   Lies!

DRIVER   He wants to move in with you!

PEASANT   Now I'm gonna hit someone!

DRIVER   To have a little blanket, a pillow, curtains…. He dreams about someone taking him in!

PEASANT   You're a snake. A damned liar.

DRIVER   He wants his fried eggs in the morning!

OLD WOMAN   Oh, and I just happen to have a little hen…. Oh…. (*Embarrassed.*)

DRIVER   What? (*To the peasant.*) And you dare … you … just after a suicide attempt … to live in a village with a lot of innocent people??

PEASANT (*shouts*)   So what? What did I say? Ah? Did I say anything? No, you just tell me, why are you carrying on like a banshee? Did I say anything?

EGNINEER   You're the one who is screeching! I'm saying it calmly. You're the one who's freaking out!

PEASANT   No, but why are you yelling, eh? Why are you yelling, I ask? Get out of here.

DRIVER   You get out of here!

PEASANT   Hey, you!

DRIVER   And who are you?!

PEASANT   Get going, will you!

DRIVER   You get going!

PEASANT   I'm a walker. I walk with my feet, like ... any other person! Get lost!

OLD WOMAN   Citizens, why are you so angry? Always angry. (*To the peasant.*) I haven't even thought about that. My house is old, of course ... but ... the village will give us everything ... building materials ... where there's a will.... Our village is friendly ... you just have to ask.

DRIVER   What's he good for? He did time.

PEASANT   I drive bulldozers.

DRIVER   That's funny! He drives bulldozers! Who needs bulldozer drivers in a village?

OLD WOMAN   I do.

DRIVER   You're completely insane, lady. You found this piece of trash on the rails and want to drag it home.

OLD WOMAN   I'm not forcing anybody to do anything. But you can stay with me, if you like. People have always wandered. Some stay, some wander on. There's a vegetable garden. The little barn can be lifted. The Tapkins can help, if need be.... The barn is crushing their currants, anyway. I'll tell them you're my nephew, don't worry.

PEASANT   Mother ... I'm, you know.... (*To Driver.*) So buddy, are you half-frozen, huh? He's such a puny little thing, isn't he?

Mother, aren't the young puny these days?

Old woman giggles.

They don't know life, but they show off! They don't walk, they ride. You should walk more, understand? Your legs are like noodles. Hey, look up there now, see the stars shining? (*Points to the sky.*) Eh-eh… (*Pulls Driver's cap down on his nose.*)

DRIVER   They're shining, but not for you…. You said it yourself. You have no shame conning an old lady.

OLD WOMAN (*motions to Peasant not to pay attention*)   It's all right! All right! All right!

Peasant straightens himself, takes his hat off, passes his hand over his shaved head.

So what do you think now?

PEASANT   Mother. I….

OLD WOMAN   What is it?

PEASANT   Let's say, if I….

OLD WOMAN   Have you made up your mind?

PEASANT   Mother, when I drink red wine, I beat people up.

OLD WOMAN   We'll manage.

DRIVER   Here we go.

PEASANT (*roars*)   Listen, mother! If these hands … in a drunken stupor … slam into a grey head!

DRIVER   Just look at him, will you. Look at him … a bandit. A real bandit.

PEASANT   I'd rather saw off my hands than hit you.

OLD WOMAN   Stop it now! All this shouting! First of all, you won't saw anything off, it's not your nature. Second, I've been beaten up before, there's nothing new in that.

PEASANT   I'll saw them off, I swear.

DRIVER   Sure, he'll saw them off. I can see it now.

PEASANT   I'll saw them off. Bit by bit.

OLD WOMAN   This isn't right, your going on like that. Just like my little goat, just as headstrong!

PEASANT   I'll find your goat.

DRIVER   Sure. He'll find it.

OLD WOMAN   You'll like him. Once you get used to him, he's funny, like a little dog. Nice.

PEASANT   I said I would. I don't like to repeat things.

OLD WOMAN   So now … shall we go or what? (*To Driver.*) No use standing about, eh? There's plenty to do, you know. It was nice meeting you. So long.

PEASANT (*to Driver*)   So long, railroad man.

DRIVER   And what about my fiver?

PEASANT   Shit! (*To Old Woman.*) Sorry.

OLD WOMAN   It's nothing! Nothing! Nothing!

PEASANT (*returning the money*)   Here. What're you looking at? I have one hundred eighty-seven rubles. Here. (*Pulls money out of his pocket.*) Little mother, I've got cash, don't worry. One hundred eighty-seven rubles.

OLD WOMAN   I don't need anything! I don't need anything!

PEASANT   Sure, sure! I know what that means, "don't need

Go!

anything!" (*They're walking.*) Sometimes it's a scarf or something else. "Don't need anything...."

DRIVER   You're leaving now, right?

OLD WOMAN   Right. It's a long way.... See over there ... where the village lights are shining?

DRIVER   Good-bye then.

OLD WOMAN   All right. You be on your way now. Or they'll scold you for stopping the train. It was nice meeting you.

DRIVER   We're all leaving then.

OLD WOMAN   It's just that you, citizen....

PEASANT   Is she talkative or what....

OLD WOMAN (*to Driver*)   You'll get on your steam train now....

DRIVER   Electric locomotive...

OLD WOMAN   On your locomotive. And get going. Your job isn't easy. You have to take people to all sorts of places.

DRIVER   But my shift's almost over. This guy knows.

PEASANT   What's this now?

DRIVER (*to Old Woman*)   I'm off to bed now.

OLD WOMAN   So go to bed. Is it warm there—in your train?

DRIVER   Sure. It wouldn't do for it to be cold! We don't want that! How could I drive the train?

OLD WOMAN   So you'll go to bed now and tomorrow it'll be a new day, you'll be riding the train with snow everywhere, all shiny. The fields are clean and beautiful now.

DRIVER   No, little mother, it's not like that. We each sleep four hours. My partner and I take turns. Our job's like that.

47

PEASANT   What does he want now, eh?

DRIVER   I told him the story of my life like a stupid idiot....

PEASANT   I don't give a damn about your life!

DRIVER   He called me names, so what? I forgave him. I just want to say that if anything goes wrong … turn him in to the police. They'll put him back in jail.

PEASANT   Hey, you!

OLD WOMAN   It's nothing! Nothing! We still have a long way to go. And you have a whole train with shiny windows … and you …you'll get married, you'll have children … why are you still hanging around?

DRIVER   Who—me?! Well, so what! (*Laughs.*) Like Pushkin said: "Cold and sun, and the day is wonderful!" (*Starts walking.*)

PEASANT (*gloomy*)   So, get going.

DRIVER   Haven't I seen enough insanity? Do they pay me a salary to deal with weirdos…? Like Pushkin said: "You're still sleeping, my beautiful friend!"

PEASANT   Go on, leave, you good for nothing....

OLD WOMAN   Come on. It's still dark.

PEASANT   All right, let's go, mother. Don't want to run into any riff-raff…. (*They leave.*)

Train passes.

CURTAIN

Translated from the Russian
*by **Nadya L. Peterson***

↪ Nina Sadur

CHARACTERS

PECHORIN

MAKSIM MAKSIMYCH

KAZBICH

GRUSHNITSKY

MARY

VERA

VERA'S HUSBAND

OLD PRINCESS LIGOVSKOY

WERNER

A CAPTAIN OF THE DRAGOONS

A MAGICIAN

BELA

A MALE ACROBAT

A FEMALE ACROBAT

OFFICERS, MEMBERS S OF THE "SPA SOCIETY," ABREKS

PROLOGUE

The Caucasus

PECHORIN   What's that?

MAKSIM MAKSIMYCH (M.M.)   A cloud over Mount Gud.

PECHORIN   No, I mean ... the whole ... picture.

M.M.   That's what it looks like when the sun sets in these parts.

PECHORIN   Does that mean the Caucasus only exist for the sake of these glorious colors?

M.M.   Who knows! Sometimes the sight makes one want to howl, sir, and at other times it grabs your heart so hard that it tears it out with the flesh.

A high mountain path on the edge of a precipice. A blizzard is in the offing.

Maksim Maksimych and Pechorin are walking on the path, followed later by Abreks.

M.M.   I've had it with this Asia! Its people and its rivers, always the same—you can't count on a thing.

PECHORIN   What do you mean?

M.M.   They're savages! Worthless! Completely hopeless! Such brutes! They have no use for education or even the most basic culture. They're robbers and beggars, sir, they never stop lying. But I'll say this, they're reckless and brave, regular daredevils!

And—you won't believe it—they know what sorrow is, just like us!

PECHORIN   Impossible! Their hearts are primitive!

M.M.   It's hard to know what their hearts are like, sir, but I dare say, if you stea … capture one of their favorite horses, in a word, if the horse is lost, the brute will die.

PECHORIN   Is this praise or reproach, Captain?

M.M.   I don't know myself. I just feel sorry for the fellow, that's all. Someone might steal his horse on a whim, but for a savage such a loss can break his heart.

PECHORIN   They're wild, savages! Thieves!

M.M.   And what thieves, sir! Fiends out of hell! It's not enough to steal a herd of horses, their men will set fire to the station, stick a knife in every soldier, and laugh the whole time, like devils on a rampage.

PECHORIN   You've completely confused me, Captain. It's all right for them to steal, but not for anyone to steal from them, because they might take it too hard?

M.M.   Sir, you are looking at it from the wrong perspective. You're from the frozen north. But here…, you see, a true man of the Caucasus with just a year in the service will start bragging: he knows the Georgian through and through, he knows the Armenian, he knows the poor Chechen, too; and the Tatars of the Transcaucasia—he'll tell you, he knows them better than himself!

PECHORIN   Would he be lying?

Pechorin: In Memoriam

M.M. He'll even go so far as to pull on some loose-fitting trousers, lie in the shade of a plane tree, and suck on a hookah. But the people are all savages. That's all there is to it.

PECHORIN Is it worth getting to know them?

M.M. I beg your pardon?

PECHORIN Can a man used to the steppes bear it this high up in the mountains?

M.M. Everywhere is God's world, sir. Will you believe it, I've been in the Caucasus for ten years now! Ten years! And I'm still in the dark!

PECHORIN Goodness, Captain, you walk these mountain paths like a native.

M.M. Oh, sir, do you see that cloud over Mount Gud? A storm is coming, and here we are, inching along the trail. If we're not to get caught, we'd better hope for more light over the Devil's Gorge![1]

PECHORIN The Devil's Gorge?

M.M. The path there is treacherous with ice. We'll get caught midway along the precipice. Just look over there! Do you see how natives make their huts—they're clinging to cliff sides. Foolhardy! What a people! Even a bird wouldn't have dared!

---

[1] "Chertova"—from the Russian words "cherta" (line) and "chert" (devil). As the protagonist of *A Hero of Our Times* explains in the original, despite the potentially ominous meaning, Chertova Dolina (damned valley), originates from the word "cherta" (line), because it crosses the former border with Georgia.

Lawless they are, but brave! Their horses are just like them—can't be broken by the likes of us.

PECHORIN   Is that really so?

M.M.   Not on their lives! It's a wilderness here! A wilderness, sir!

> *A man on horseback flashes by. A horse neighs. The man on horseback screams wildly, in a high-pitched tone.*

M.M.   The storm has driven the Abreks this way. A bad sign.

> *It gets dark quickly with the approach of a blizzard. The Abreks hurry past like shadows, bypassing the travelers.*

PECHORIN   A blizzard! What air! It's wonderful to breathe, to feel it against the skin!

M.M.   Well, my beauty, you can't spread out here. Listen to that howling! You're pent up in a narrow pass, it's not like Saratov and the steppes.

PECHORIN   It's snowing! Blow, blow your hardest! How refreshing it feels on my face.

M.M.   Look how it's thrashing in the canyons. See it twisting and raging. Oh, sir, this is no place to get caught. How many times have I said—stop staring at those cursed sunsets! And I'm such a softie myself! Thanks to all that staring at sunsets, we're caught now! Everything is treacherous here, sir! This is Asia!

> *A light can be seen in the blizzard. It stops in mid-air and hovers in the snow.*
>
> *One can see that it is a hut, and in it, by a fire, sits a mountaineer in the fetal position.*
>
> *The hut appears to float on the edge of the precipice.*

Pechorin: In Memoriam ∽

M.M.   We have to do something, sir, quick, duck into that hut over
there! Careful you don't miss it!

> *They step gingerly into the hut. It floats over the edge of the
> precipice.*
>
> *Abreks dart around the path in the blizzard....*
>
> *Maksim Maksimych, Pechorin, Kazbich in the hut.*

M.M.   Hey, you, sheepskin hat! Can't you greet your guests?

> *Silence.*

Make yourself comfortable, sir. In the meantime, I'll start the
tea. I make very good tea.

PECHORIN   Something smells—rancid—in here.

M.M.   It's the cheese. And sheepskins. (*To the mountaineer.*) What
are you doing, pal? Your fire is barely alive. (*Stirs the fire.*)

PECHORIN   Is he even alive himself?

M.M.   Don't mind him. He'll answer when he feels like it.

PECHORIN   Do you know him?

M.M.   I don't think so. But I know their habits. See how still he
is? He's twisted himself up into a little ball and doesn't seem
to breathe, but his eyes, there, back, behind the rags—his eyes
are roaming! (*To the mountaineer.*) Don't you dare start acting
up, brother! I can be pretty harsh! See—there's a storm outside,
it's about to blow your hut into the abyss and you haven't even
made a proper fire.... You call this order? No! (*To Pechorin.*)
Only my back's gone stiff in this wind, sir. (*To the mountaineer.*)

Brother, toss me a skin –a thick one. (*The mountaineer throws him one.*) Thanks, pal—otherwise, I might not be able stand up straight by morning.

PECHORIN   What about the storm?

M.M.   It's going to last all night. (*Looks at the path through a crack in the hut.*) Such bandits, they're darting around, on the prowl! We found shelter just in time. These are such cut-throats, sir; they're not your average brutes, they're Abreks!

PECHORIN   Real Chechens?

M.M.   As real as they get! Such people—God forbid! A Chechen is your worst savage! He understands absolutely nothing! Go at him with everything you've got—he still won't understand! He'll be riddled with bullets, as full of holes as a sieve, but he's still brandishing his sword, the numbskull! These skins have wondrous healing powers. Wrap yourself in a rawhide skin, and it will make you feel so ... I can't even describe it.... They can cure rheumatism like it's nothing at all; when you're inside one, it feels like you're napping in your mother's womb, as if you'd never been born into this world.

PECHORIN   Really? Let me try one... (*He wraps himself in a skin.*)

M.M.   How does it feel?

PECHORIN   Nice.

M.M.   Just nice?

PECHORIN   There is no more draft, at least. Don't let it bother you, Captain, I probably haven't gotten used to it yet, that's all.

M.M.   I know: our huts are squalid, our speech is unpolished, and

Pechorin: In Memoriam

in here there's an acrid reek of smoke, and you, with your white skin, your city pallor…. What kind of soldiers are they sending us! Holy mother of God! It makes you want to cry!… but at least the faces are Russian.

PECHORIN   Why don't you go home then?

M.M.   You see, sir, I'm alone in the world. I'll stay here as a junior captain until the day I die, unless, of course, one of those wretches takes it into his head to stab me…. Such people, really, such blockheads! I don't have a place of my own back home, and who wants to skulk around other people's corners in old age…. I like these skins though; once you curl up in one, your heart feels so peaceful and quiet, it's as if you'd never been born.

PECHORIN (*wrapping himself tightly*)   You're right, it is rather peaceful.

M.M.   Chuckle all you want, sir, there's a reason why these people wrap themselves up in them. Look around—they're sewn up in sheepskins, head to toe! What can you say? They live right below the clouds and are always in a hurry, rushing God knows where and doing things frantically, headlong. Sometimes I don't know whether they actually exist on these heights or this old soldier is seeing things.

PECHORIN   Could it be that they haven't been born yet?

M.M.   Beg your pardon?

PECHORIN   Perhaps the Almighty has dropped them here, into these mountains, before their time….

M.M.   Is that what they teach you in the capital these days?

PECHORIN   Just an idle thought! Don't be offended, Captain.

M.M.   Do you want to get a good look at him, sir?

PECHORIN   No, I don't.

M.M.   Sir, you ought to!

PECHORIN   He's unconscious. How can you shake him back to life?

M.M.   That's easy, sir! Hey, brother! (*Speaks in Kazbich's tongue.*)

Kazbich turns toward the fire.

Don't move!!

PECHORIN   What's the matter?

M.M.   Sir! It's him! Him!

PECHORIN   Who?

M.M.   How you've hidden yourself, brother! You thought we wouldn't recognize you wrapped up like that! Congratulations, sir, you behold the most inveterate thief in the whole Caucasus.

PECHORIN   No!

M.M.   I know him personally! He and I are *kunaks*, good buddies in their language. Kazbich!

KAZBICH   Whot?

M.M.   You see?

PECHORIN   A living Chechen? So close?

M.M.   Most certainly! The hat, the dagger—everything! And you say—before their time! But he—here he is! He makes even the Caucasus weep! Even the Caucasus!

PECHORIN   And he' such a skinny, unimposing little man.

M.M.   That's the whole point—he just looks that way. He's a force of nature, worse than an avalanche! Worse than a waterfall! You'll see!

Pechorin: In Memoriam

PECHORIN Don't provoke him, Captain.

M.M. Don't worry, sir! I know how to deal with his kind. Kazbich! Tell me, where have you been?

KAZBICH Whot?

M.M. There you see, sir, he was beyond the Don. You are about to find out what he was doing there! Kazbich, tell me, were you stealing horses beyond the Don? Confess!

KAZBICH Whot?

M.M. You see!

PECHORIN He's insolent!

M.M. Very! A thief, through and through! (*To Kazbich.*) No-no-no! I don't want to know about such shenanigans!... So how many did you steal?

KAZBICH Whot?

M.M. What do you think?

PECHORIN A chatty fellow.

M.M. Sir, he's such a thief, such a thief, the father of all thieves! After all, this is Kazbich! Kazbich! Hey, brother, you're wounded. Your shoulder, there under the rags, your shoulder is bleeding. Tell me, Kazbich, who hurt you?

KAZBICH An infidel.

M.M. Here, put this on your wound.

KAZBICH Whot?

M.M. Stop hopping around! I'm not going to eat you! There! (*Closes the wound.*)

PECHORIN Be careful, he's wild, you know....

M.M.   Right you are, sir! You won't believe this—he'd stab you in the back at the drop of a hat!

PECHORIN   I believe it very well!

M.M.   Sir, a blade in the back is the blow of a thug!

PECHORIN   That's something you and I will never understand.

M.M.   He's a true savage, sir! See how his eyes glare at us? It's as if he were going to eat us. But he's got such a horse!

PECHORIN   What do I want with his horse?

M.M.   Go ahead, sir, ask him about his horse! Hey, Kazbich! Go ahead, sir!

PECHORIN   What for? What's the point?

M.M.   Just wait till you see what he tells you. Ask him, sir!

PECHORIN   All right. Hey, Kazbich! How's your horse?

KAZBICH   Whot?

PECHORIN   Just as I thought.

M.M.   Do you have a fine horse, Kazbich? Oh, you do, I know.

KAZBICH   Karagyoz!

PECHORIN   He understands!

M.M.   He understands everything, sir! Tell us, Kazbich, is your horse named Karagyoz?

KAZBICH   Whot?!

M.M.   Look at that, he's already put out! Can't even ask him a question! Don't you make me angry, brother! Such a blockhead. Answer the question! Is your horse happy and healthy?

KAZBICH   Whot?! Whot?!

Pechorin: In Memoriam ✍

M.M.   Dzhigit![2]

PECHORIN   Dzhigit. Good night.

> *Nighttime. Everyone's asleep. Pechorin slips out of the hut.*
> *The neighing of a horse is heard. The hut—a cage made out of*
> *twigs—is rocking over the precipice. Kazbich is darting*
> *about inside.*
>
> *Pechorin is standing on the cliff on the other side of the precipice.*
> *The horse is with him. M.M. is standing on the old trail, on the*
> *opposite side.*

M.M.   Now what's going to happen! Now what's going to happen? What should we do? Oh, dear God! Such misfortune!

PECHORIN   Come now, Maksim Maksimovich! You're exaggerating! Everything will be fine!

M.M.   How can it be fine? To bring a Chechen to his knees, weeping? This is not something they can do!

PECHORIN   So what, now he knows how to.

M.M.   Oh, sir, oh, such an evil deed! Why?

PECHORIN   It's a fine horse. I noticed it back during the sunset.

M.M.   A rare, rare steed! What now? Beautiful, smart, and a real devil—a thief's horse! You won't manage him.

PECHORIN   I will give it a try.

M.M.   Eh, sir, the horse won't submit.

PECHORIN   Yes, it will!

M.M.   No, it won't! It can't understand Russian. It bites!

---

[2]   Turkic for skilled horseman, a term frequently used in the Caucasus.

PECHORIN   I will teach it. I will feed it sugar. I will comb its forelock.

M.M.   Its legs are like strings, with tiny hooves, it's definitely a mountain horse; it's trained to fly over precipices and jump across treacherous rocks; it will break its legs in our lowlands.

PECHORIN   And so?

M.M.   Sir!

PECHORIN   What is it, Maksim Maksimych?

M.M.   Sir, it would have been kinder to kill him.

PECHORIN   He's only a savage.

M.M.   All the more cruel. He won't understand why his horse is gone, but he's still here.

PECHORIN   He's a thief! He'll stab a man in the back.

M.M.   Yes! Yes!! But where is his Karagyoz? Kazbich is here, but Karagyoz is gone!

PECHORIN   So what! He'd steal an entire herd. A horse-thief!

M.M.   A penniless wretch! A blockhead! But no horse! No matter where you look, the animal's gone!

PECHORIN   He can steal, kill, and ride off—and won't bat an eyelash.

M.M.   Yes! Yes!! He'll ride off! But lo, the horse is gone!

PECHORIN   You amuse me. You'll be first to get stabbed from behind. The minute you turn your back.

M.M.   Then I won't turn it! I know—he's wild! I'll be on my guard! Now, all of a sudden, he has no horse. He had a horse, and now he's alone.

Pechorin: In Memoriam

PECHORIN   Oh, Maksim Maksimych, I'd return the horse, if even for your sake, but there's no going back; and his feelings—it's ridiculous! He's running around on all fours, growling, eating raw meat, and his face is swarthy. What feelings?

M.M.   It's sordid, sordid and primitive. There are no decent feelings here. How can they develop? From the moment you're born, all you see are mountains, fights, rocks, everything's plummeting, thundering, the eagles are clapping their wings, bullets are flying! By the time you make sense of anything, it's time to die. How is he going to make it without this horse of his, without Karagyoz?! How is he going to make it without Karagyoz? Now, do you understand?

PECHORIN   One can live with the most unbearable sorrow! One can live very well. And even get used to it. And even be bored by it. And still live.

M.M.   But the savage doesn't understand sorrow. After all, he's a dzhigit—a horseman. He's been riding from the cradle. Now, just like that—snap!—his entire life is gone!

PECHORIN (*looking into the abyss*)   So much snow has blown into your Devil's Gorge. You won't believe it: "And sparkling in the sun, the snow lies!" This is not the Caucasus; this is Saratov, this is Tambov province. Just like that—snap!—and it's over.

M.M.   Dear God! What's your name, sir!

PECHORIN (*falling into the abyss*)   A-ah! Call me Pechorin....

M.M.   Well, hello, Grigory Aleksandrovich.

ACT I

Scene 1: Officer's quarters.
Pechorin, Grushnitsky, later Werner, Vera, officers.
Grushnitsky is looking in a mirror. Pechorin lies on his bed.
Officers periodically pop in to take things from their nightstands.

PECHORIN (*his stomach hurts*) Can it be due to the effect of the waters?

GRUSHNITSKY You're a materialist, Pechorin.

PECHORIN It is due to the effect of the waters.

GRUSHNITSKY You see the nasty side of everything. Have you got any scent?

PECHORIN What for? You simply reek of rose pomade, as it is.

GRUSHNITSKY Never mind. Give it here. (*Trying on his new officer's coat.*) How do you like it?

PECHORIN Flatten the lapels. Turn around. The back is scrunched up.

GRUSHNITSKY Where, where?

PECHORIN Werner has prescribed two glasses daily. Maybe mineral waters don't work for me? After all, I do have a weak stomach. Two glasses!

GRUSHNITSKY They call him Mephistopheles around here, you know.

PECHORIN Werner also prescribed me the baths. Have you tried them yet?

GRUSHNITSKY Pechorin, those baths are full of decrepit old people. Let's ride to the Hollow instead!

Pechorin: In Memoriam

PECHORIN   Have you ever tried sweating it out in the Ermolov bathhouse? Many people swear by it.

GRUSHNITSKY   Of course I haven't! If you want to be serious — I could be killed any day. As could you, of course. Do you believe that the proximity of death heightens the senses?

PECHORIN   The Old Princess.

GRUSHNITSKY   What about the Old Princess?

PECHORIN   The Old Princess sweats it out in the Ermolov bathhouse.

GRUSHNITSKY   Do you mean Princess Ligovskoy?

PECHORIN   Daily. At ten in the morning.

GRUSHNITSKY   How do you know?

Vera peeks out.

VERA   Understand, only there, only at the Princess's, will we be able to see each other. The Princess is a distant aunt of mine. You have to make her acquaintance. Only there, only there can we see each other. You must, you must make the Princess's acquaintance. Promise me you will make the Princess's acquaintance.

Vera disappears.

PECHORIN   Oh, what tedium!

GRUSHNITSKY   So, what about the Old Princess? What about the Old Princess, I ask?

PECHORIN   How should I know? She sweats it out! You're the one who's acquainted with the family!

GRUSHNITSKY   Would you like me to introduce you? I'll arrange it! Even after something like that!

PECHORIN   Spare me. And what do you mean by *that*?

GRUSHNITSKY   Admit that you want me to! Admit it!

PECHORIN   I have no energy for anything. Absolutely none. There's a shooting pain in my side and my stomach is bloated. Where's Werner? Werner!

GRUSHNITSKY   You shouldn't have made Mary angry.

PECHORIN   So intimate already—Mary!

GRUSHNITSKY   Of course not! She's nobility. She's proud. To them, I'm only a rough and ready military man. (*Turning around in front of the mirror.*) Damned Jew, the sleeves are too narrow. Do I have time to get them fixed before the ball?

PECHORIN   What ball? When?

GRUSHNITSKY   I swear, it's like you're from another world! It's today, in the restaurant. Although it's by subscription. Put your name down! You must!

PECHORIN   You don't even know how to dance a mazurka. I'll have to invite the Young Princess.

GRUSHNITSKY   No way, no way! She'll never dance with you. She's angry with you!

PECHORIN   Impossible!

GRUSHNITSKY   I didn't want to say so, but she doesn't think much of you.

PECHORIN   But we aren't even acquainted! Oh, there it goes again! Call the doctor!

GRUSHNITSKY   She says that you have a disagreeable gaze.

PECHORIN   Me? Why would she say that?

GRUSHNITSKY   Impudent. Can you imagine, that's exactly what she said—he's got an impudent gaze!

PECHORIN   She couldn't have!

GRUSHNITSKY   Pechorin, you must admit that you are too impolite with the use of your lorgnette.

PECHORIN   Oh, the Muscovite Princess! Someone dared to point the lens at her!

GRUSHNITSKY   Deliberately. Fixedly. Mary—she's an angel. You won't believe it, but her soul is sublime. Yes, and she also says you don't think well of yourself.

PECHORIN   That much is true. (*Looks at Grushnitsky through his lorgnette.*)

GRUSHNITSKY   (*turning around*)   Give it here. (*Tries the same.*) How do you do it?

Fiddling with the lorgnette. They inspect imaginary ladies.

PECHORIN   (*short of breath from playing with the lorgnette*)   I must say, the Young Princess Mary is looking very pretty.

GRUSHNITSKY   Incredible woman! Incredible!

PECHORIN   She has velvety eyes. Yes, velvety is the right word. The upper and lower lashes are so long that the pupils don't reflect sunlight. This makes them seem lusterless.

GRUSHNITSKY   Don't speak of her, Pechorin! I won't be held accountable!

PECHORIN   I like eyes like that: they're so soft, they seem to stroke you. And her teeth, are they white?

GRUSHNITSKY   Why do you ask?

PECHORIN   It's very important for teeth to be white! It's a pity I haven't seen her smile.

GRUSHNITSKY   You talk of a pretty woman as you would of an English horse.

PECHORIN   And her feet.... Have you noticed how the English boot fits the foot so closely?

GRUSHNITSKY   I confess I haven't.

PECHORIN   Most important is that her ankle be so thin you can circle it with your fingers, like this. And, then, the outline of her thigh....

GRUSHNITSKY   Pechorin! You're aware of my love for her, right?

PECHORIN   I am.

GRUSHNITSKY   Remember, there is a living heart that beats beneath this coat.

PECHORIN   You're wearing an officer's coat, albeit an unfinished one.... I feel sad. My stomach hurts. Where is the doctor?

GRUSHNITSKY   Pechorin, don't joke about my love. You have a spiteful tongue. I also have a spiteful tongue. Perhaps that's what's made us friends—our tendency to notice vulgarity in others. Is it ten yet?

PECHORIN   Why?

GRUSHNITSKY   I promised the Young Princess to adjust her telescope. She wants to have a closer look at Elbrus.

Pechorin: In Memoriam ✆

PECHORIN   Elbrus! You don't mean it! Elbrus!

GRUSHNITSKY   Do you want to remain my friend?

PECHORIN   I do. Elbrus....

GRUSHNITSKY   Do you?

PECHORIN   I do.

GRUSHNITSKY   Well then. You should stop avoiding society. You should stop running away from it. They say you spend hours riding in the steppe. I don't understand.

PECHORIN   I ride for my amusement.

GRUSHNITSKY   Amusement?

PECHORIN   My amusement, I swear!

GRUSHNITSKY   You've just ridden your third horse to death.

PECHORIN   That's because my horses are weak. But I have just procured a wondrous black stallion. It belonged to a Chechen, a thief. Oh, such a horse! Would you believe I love that horse more than life itself? You know, fluttering nostrils and eyes like Bela's....

GRUSHNITSKY   Like whose?

PECHORIN   Never mind. A Chechen name slipped out. A random one.

GRUSHNITSKY   Pechorin, don't tease me!

PECHORIN   Wait. Sometimes I think that horse misses its owner with a fatal, unbearable longing. Imagine, it refuses to take salt from my hands! And here you are—Elbrus!

GRUSHNITSKY   I pity you, Pechorin. You could have been visiting the Princess. It's one of the most agreeable houses here.

PECHORIN   The most agreeable house is my own. Why doesn't the doctor come?

GRUSHNITSKY   Confess that you're sorry. Listen, perhaps it can still be arranged.

PECHORIN   What nonsense! I shall be at the Old Princess's tomorrow!

GRUSHNITSKY   We shall see!

PECHORIN   You shall see! And to oblige you, I shall flirt with the Young Princess.

GRUSHNITSKY   She won't even speak to you.

PECHORIN   You know what? I'll wager she doesn't know that you've just been promoted to officer. She thinks you've been degraded to the ranks.

GRUSHNITSKY   Perhaps. It doesn't matter.

PECHORIN   You don't know the average Russian woman, Grushnitsky. They love platonically. They love the dream. The smoke. They have pink fog before their eyes. They're dangerous for young men, especially for wounded officers. More dangerous than the Circassian, friend.

GRUSHNITSKY   What's there to fear?

PECHORIN   The average Russian woman is capable of tearing one apart for the sake of her platonics.

GRUSHNITSKY   Tear me to pieces, just like that? With her sharp little claws?

PECHORIN   Yes, to pieces. If you give off the scent of fresh blood.

GRUSHNITSKY   But I'm brave!

Pechorin: In Memoriam

PECHORIN   Brave. Yes, brave. Anyway, this is all nonsense.

Enter Doctor Werner

Doctor! Your waters aren't working!

GRUSHNITSKY   No, wait. What did you mean? Are you questioning my courage?

PECHORIN   Not at all…. Oh, another cramp….

WERNER (*to Pechorin*)   Show me your tongue…. Breathe…. Now hold your breath. I recommend a good sweat.

PECHORIN   Do you think it might help?

WERNER   No. But still, I'm going to prescribe the Ermolov baths.

Enter Vera

VERA   Tell me, do you find it amusing to torture me? I ought to hate you. Ever since we've known each other, you have caused me nothing but suffering…. But come, come to the Ermolov bathhouse. You realize, it's a perfect pretext. The Old Princess is my distant aunt; only there, in the steam, only there can we see each other, only there. There is steam there, and there is fog, only there can we….

GRUSHNITSKY   But doctor! These baths are for elderly people.

PECHORIN (*To Werner*)   Daily? At ten in the morning?

WERNER   Daily. At ten in the morning. (*To Grushnitsky.*) But I cannot congratulate you.

GRUSHNITSKY   Why not?

WERNER   Because a soldier's coat is very becoming on you, but the uniform of an infantry officer, made by a provincial tailor in a watering place like this, will not confer any glamour.

GRUSHNITSKY   Why not?

WERNER   Up to now you were an exception; now you will come under the general rule.

GRUSHNITSKY   Go on, go on, doctor! "Epaulets, epaulets, your little stars glisten!" No, today I am happy! I am completely happy!

PECHORIN   And your uniform isn't even ready yet!

GRUSHNITSKY   Oh, right. But it will be ready in time for the ball. However, I'm late. (*Takes off his uniform.*) Good bye, doctor.

WERNER   Good bye.

PECHORIN   Where are you off to?

GRUSHNITSKY   To Elbrus! (*Hurries out.*)

PECHORIN   Did you hear that? Elbrus!

WERNER   I don't like your color.

PECHORIN   What a fool!

WERNER   I think your liver is acting up. Let's have a look at your stomach. (*Palpating his abdomen.*) Does it hurt here?

PECHORIN   No.

WERNER   Here?

PECHORIN   No.

WERNER   How about here?

PECHORIN   Oh, doctor, of course it hurts if you do that!

WERNER   Your liver is fine. But that hint of yellow in your face.... I don't like it. I don't understand your organism. You are as healthy as an ox. Why are you wasting away?

PECHORIN   To hell with my organism, Doctor!

Pechorin: In Memoriam

WERNER   Yes?

PECHORIN   Give me some news.

WERNER (*after a pause*)   What news would you like?

PECHORIN   Is there really so much to choose from? What about the flies? Don't the flies bother you?

WERNER   The flies do bother me. And there are two items of news about the waters.

PECHORIN   Don't tell me!

WERNER   No?

PECHORIN   You and I are two intelligent people, aren't we?

WERNER   If you say so.

PECHORIN   We know in advance how things will end up. Am I correct? I am correct. Don't bother to answer.

WERNER   The first piece of news. There have been inquiries about you.

PECHORIN   The Old Princess!

WERNER   How do you know it wasn't the Young Princess?

PECHORIN   The Young Princess asked about Grushnitsky.

WERNER   You have a great talent for reasoning. The Young Princess is convinced that the young man who just left has been degraded to the ranks for a duel!

PECHORIN   You didn't tell her that he was a cadet?

WERNER   I did not.

PECHORIN   We have the beginning of a plot. The denouement of this comedy will be amusing.

WERNER   I have a presentiment that poor Grushnitsky is going to be your victim.

PECHORIN   Go on with your story, doctor! The Old Princess!

WERNER   The Old Princess. Her digestion is excellent, but there's something wrong with her blood.

PECHORIN   Go on.

WERNER   She is fond of risqué anecdotes; she says improper things herself. She told me that her daughter was as pure as an angel. What do I care? She is very fond of young men. Her daughter, on the contrary, looks at them with contempt. The daughter knows algebra.

PECHORIN   Knows what?

WERNER   And English. That's the Moscow fashion these days.

PECHORIN   Tell me!

WERNER   So should I arrange the Ermolov baths for you?

PECHORIN   The second piece of news, doctor!

WERNER   A young lady has arrived. Blonde. Regular features. She has a consumptive complexion, however. The husband is old.

PECHORIN   Old husband? Is she pretty?

WERNER   Incredibly so! She has a little mole on her cheek.

PECHORIN   A little mole!

WERNER   Let me check your heart. (*Listening to his heart.*) She's someone you know!

PECHORIN   Indeed. She's a woman I once loved. I loved her. Her alone. She may be the only woman I have ever loved. Yes, the mole, the husband, it adds up, I loved her and only her from a young age….

Pechorin: In Memoriam

WERNER   Well.

PECHORIN   Doctor, when you see her, speak of me in as unkindly a way as you can.

WERNER   As you wish.

PECHORIN   I am made in a stupid way. I forget nothing. Nothing!

Scene 2: Grushnitsky and Mary in the bushes.
Pechorin steals up, eavesdropping. Somewhere nearby
the Ermolov bath is letting out steam, and Old Princess Ligovskoy
is swimming in it.

Episode 1

Grushnitsky, Mary, later Pechorin.

GRUSHNITSKY   What is Russia to me? A country where thousands of people look on me with contempt because they're richer than I am—whereas here—a rough soldier's coat has not kept me from making your acquaintance….

MARY   On the contrary….

GRUSHNITSKY   My life here will flow by quickly and unobserved, with a great deal of noise, under the gunfire of savages; and God grant me but once a year the radiant glance of a young lady, that velvety glance that seems to be stroking a man, which drives him crazy, or may a Chechen bullet cut my life short, Princess!

MARY   Oh, no!

GRUSHNITSKY What is my life? My mother. A small village in the steppe…. Ah, the Russian steppe, Princess! As a child, I used to run wild there, over its vast expanses—silence, the blue sky, the hot haze of the scorched steppe, and nothing but the whistling of gophers….

MARY I once visited a village. I enjoyed it very much.

GRUSHNITSKY But what I am saying! You are a proud Muscovite. I am an army brute. A penniless soldier from the steppes.

MARY Are you trying to put me off?

GRUSHNITSKY Princess! I wouldn't dream of it! I'm not worthy to stand in your presence! Even to look at you!

MARY But I have come, haven't I! I've come!

GRUSHNITSKY My only excuse is that I may be dead tomorrow; I could lose my head, together with…. What can I say? Yes, I'm a brute, Princess, but I'm the product of a brutish country; be that as it may, it's a bitter joy to be here with you—and I relish it.

MARY Tell me, is it frightening to be in a battle?

GRUSHNITSKY No.

MARY No?

GRUSHNITSKY No.

MARY And … and killing, isn't that frightening either?

GRUSHNITSKY No.

MARY No?

GRUSHNITSKY Yes, no.

MARY How strange.

GRUSHNITSKY It is strange. But in war, things move so fast that there's no time to understand or feel anything. But, Princess, why do you want to know about that?

MARY   I find it very interesting.

GRUSHNITSKY   Trust me, Princess, war is such filth.

MARY   There are so many wounded officers here. I never knew Russia had so many cripples.

GRUSHNITSKY   What is Russia to me!

MARY   A country where thousands of cripples…. (*Looking around.*) Here, at the waters, everyone is afraid of the Circassians.

GRUSHNITSKY   Oh, Mary! You have a soldier to keep you safe!

MARY   I know, Monsieur Grushnitsky.

They kiss. Pechorin stumbles in.

Mon Dieu, des Circassiens!

GRUSHNITSKY   Halt! Hands up!

PECHORIN (*speaking French*)   Ne craignez rien, madame—je ne suis pas plus dangereux que votre chevalier!

MARY   It's you … you…. Why the sheepskin hat?

PECHORIN   I enjoy dressing like a Circassian.

MARY   Ah!

GRUSHNITSKY   Where did you drop in from?

PECHORIN   I was on my way to the waters. Oh dear, what a blunder! I'm despondent: I have managed to upset the Moscow Princess again.

MARY   Oh no, it's just that you half startled me to death.

PECHORIN   So much the worse for me. Farewell! (*Throws himself into the Ermolov bath.*)

MARY   Where did he disappear to, that strange gentleman?

GRUSHNITSKY   That's the way he always is. Princess, may I dare ask, may I be so bold....

MARY   Yes, Monsieur officier.

GRUSHNITSKY   There's only one excuse for my insolence—war. Even if your answer is unfavorable, a Chechen bullet will find my chest and bring comfort....

MARY   But I ... I haven't even answered you yet!

GRUSHNITSKY   Princess....

MAY. Yes?

GRUSHNITSKY   I beseech you, please sing to me.

MARY   Oh, that! (*Sings.*)

Episode 2

Old Princess Ligovskoy and Pechorin are swimming
in the Ermolov bath. Steam.

OLD PRINCESS   Who is this young man?

PECHORIN   Pechorin.

OLD PRINCESS   He's handsome.

PECHORIN   Whatever you say.

OLD PRINCESS   Is he the one from Petersburg?

PECHORIN   The very one.

OLD PRINCESS   I know quite a few of his aunts. Why does he shun my house? My house is the most agreeable one here, at the waters.

PECHORIN   They say he likes solitude.

OLD PRINCESS   That's my daughter singing. Princess Mary. She has the heart of an angel.

PECHORIN   She has black eyes.

OLD PRINCESS   Do you know that racy tale about the young French tutor who mixes up the bedrooms?

PECHORIN   Why, yes. I do.

OLD PRINCESS   This Pechorin is a complete savage. He doesn't even introduce himself.

PECHORIN   He ended up in the mother's bedroom one night instead of the daughter's.

OLD PRINCESS   Oh, to be young.... What does it feel like? I've forgotten. What are the feelings of the young? What do they sing about?

PECHORIN   He's a savage because he detests people. He detests people because he brings them nothing but misery.

OLD PRINCESS (*laughing*)   Once he realized his mistake by touch, he got so scared he wet his pants. That's a Frenchie for you! (*Laughs.*)

PECHORIN   Be careful, madam, it gets deep here.

OLD PRINCESS   Don't worry, I'm a good swimmer!

PECHORIN   He is young but old. He doesn't remember what a young man feels. The force of nature? Is that all? Who is that singing over there?

OLD PRINCESS   My daughter Mary. Princess Mary. From Moscow.

PECHORIN   She has such a fresh voice! He'll start visiting your house. He'll ruin everyone.

OLD PRINCESS   We shall see.

PECHORIN   He will, as he always does, and only for the sake of a single short-lived pleasure: for novelty.

OLD PRINCESS   That remains to be seen.

PECHORIN   For the sake of an added bitterness to his life. One more sour drop.

OLD PRINCESS   Let him come visit.

Episode 3

*A gap in a grapevine-covered wall. There is a flame in the opening.
In the flame stands Vera. Across from her—Pechorin.*

VERA   You, you, oh, it's you! I can't believe my eyes; I can't believe my senses; but still, it's you!

PECHORIN   Vera!

VERA   Listen, I'm always chilly. I'm tormented by bouts of fever and chills, chills, then fever, then chills again: I stagger, I sweat, I cough.

PECHORIN   Vera, are you here by chance or have you followed me?

VERA   I see you through a haze of heat, as if in flames. I keep thinking you're about to dissolve like a gray mist. Speak to me at least—I want to hear your voice!

PECHORIN   Seeing you after so many years makes me sad, Vera.

VERA   Perhaps I shall be dead soon. I feel myself getting weaker by the day. I am wasting away. Look at these hands. They are so desiccated that the rings and bracelets slide off. Do you remember these hands? Come here! (*Fit of coughing.*)

PECHORIN   You must be very ill.

VERA   Yes, I can't think of a future life. I think only of you. Of you.

PECHORIN   Vera, nobody has ever understood me like you. Should you be telling me these things?

VERA   We haven't seen each other for a long time. Did you recognize me, did you? Tell me, did you recognize me? We both have changed in many ways.

PECHORIN   Does that mean you no longer love me?

VERA   You'll ruin me. I know it, you'll ruin me! Never mind, I'd sacrifice everything to be near you, to see you, except … I have to keep my reputation. For the sake of my son. For the sake of his inheritance. But listen, I don't want you to meet my husband.

PECHORIN   He is old, isn't he? Old?

VERA   Tell me, have I changed a lot? Tell me, do you remember me, do you remember me just as I've remembered you through all these years? Tell me, did you recognize me? I've become so thin, so frighteningly, irrecoverably thin, and I know: this hideous redness on my cheeks scares and repels people. Listen, I'm coughing blood.

PECHORIN   Your husband!

VERA   He's too old to notice anything.

PECHORIN   Vera, listen to me. We've known each other since childhood. You know all my weaknesses: spite, envy, vindictiveness.

VERA   But I also know your strengths: you are intelligent, you are handsome, you long for love no matter what, you always, deliriously, long for nothing but love!

PECHORIN   Vera! You're the only woman I can't deceive. My heart is cold. I'm not interested in happiness. I'm not interested in passion. It's over.

VERA   You know I'm your slave; I was never able to make you like me, and for this I'm punished—you'll stop loving me. Oh, I beseech you, don't torment me again with painful doubts and feigned coldness, I think only of you….

PECHORIN   Sometimes I understand the vampire. I feel an insatiable desire to swallow up the sufferings and joys of others: it is the food that nurtures my heart.

VERA   Don't speak to me of passion. I'm too weak, I feel as if my life is draining away drop by drop, rolling off my fingertips, drip-drop…. I can't keep you close to me; my fingers, my hands, my chest are failing…. I have a thick, burning feeling beneath my heart, right here. It's as if I am oppressed by an unknown longing; at times it hurts me just to take a breath!

PECHORIN   Vera, passion is only an idea. It's the youth of one's heart; and whoever expects to keep it alive over a lifetime is deluded.

VERA   Pechorin….

PECHORIN   Yes….

VERA   Pechorin, Pechorin, Pechorin. How unhappy you are. You're concealing your sorrows, Pechorin. And the sound of your name! In the heart of every woman it awakens a vague trepidation, Pechorin. A drink! I need to drink! My mouth is always dry.

PECHORIN   A gypsy once foretold my death at the hands of a wicked wife. Since then, I've had an insuperable fear of marriage. But still, I'm drawn to women more than anything in this world.

VERA   Men are indifferent to the delights of a glance, of a hand-shake.... Whereas I—I swear to you—the sound of your voice evokes in me such bliss, the most ardent of kisses could not replace it.

PECHORIN   Bliss. It is akin to happiness. And what is happiness but sated pride? My greatest pleasure is to subjugate others to my will. It's not limitless power I want. Why should I? I have servants and money.

VERA   I know! I know you through and through. But promise me to visit the Old Princess.

PECHORIN   You have my word, Vera. I shall visit the Old Princess.

VERA   And promise me even to court the Young Princess.

PECHORIN   Why?!

VERA   Because ... because she is pretty, very pretty, and it's the normal, vital, natural thing to do.

PECHORIN   All right.

VERA   But still, there is inexplicable delight in loving you even as I am dying.

Nina Sadur

Episode 4

The Ball

Spa society. The hall of a restaurant transformed into a hall for the Club of the Nobility. Dancing. Observers stand around in groups.

GRUSHNITSKY   Pechorin, I adore balls! I am so happy! Tell me, how does my new coat become me?

PECHORIN   Like a saddle on a cow!

GRUSHNITSKY   Enough sulking! Dance! What kind of a man are you! Don't forget, we may die tomorrow!

PECHORIN   Look, such beautiful feet!

GRUSHNITSKY   Pechorin, I confess....

PECHORIN   Wait! There, again! How attractive the women are! Attractive, indeed!

GRUSHNITSKY   Just to a friend.... Only one woman exists for me.

PECHORIN   Oh?

GRUSHNITSKY   Pechorin, don't make fun of me. I love the Princess Mary to distraction! To distraction!

PECHORIN   It's not for dolts like us to drink tea! We'll have to settle for the sidelines. Look, the Princess!

GRUSHNITSKY   The Princess! Did you see how she looked at me? Did you see that glance?

PECHORIN   I no longer dare use my lorgnette! And without it, I can't see a thing. Thank goodness.

GRUSHNITSKY   I'm going to dance with the Princess all night. I'll be with her till I drop!

Pechorin: In Memoriam

PECHORIN   Well, I hope you trip on your own legs!

GRUSHNITSKY   You heartless cynic! (*Rushes off.*)

***

Old Princess, Young Princess, later Grushnitsky

OLD PRINCESS   Mary, you're not well!

MARY   I'm fine, Mama.

OLD PRINCESS   I can see, Mary, you're not well!

MARY   Mama, you mustn't overdo it with the sulfur baths!

OLD PRINCESS   The steam softens the bones, Mary. The sulfur purges one's ailments.

MARY   I, rather, feel that the sulfur baths "soften the brain." (*Speaking English.*)

OLD PRINCESS   Mary, don't you even look at that Grushnitsky. He's not an appropriate suitor.

MARY   He is simply a poor, wretched man, Mama, nothing else.

OLD PRINCESS   All of Russia is wretched and poor, my child!

They are joined by Grushnitsky.

Monsieur officier!

GRUSHNITSKY   The entire officer corps is at your service, madam.

OLD PRINCESS   Those young men in bandages covered with medals—who are they?

GRUSHNITSKY   Those are the Dragoons, madam. They are imps and devils, but such lions!

OLD PRINCESS   Lions? But that's commendable!

GRUSHNITSKY (*to Mary*)   Princess, dare I ask….

MARY   I won't sing again!

GRUSHNITSKY   You promised me a dance, Princess!

MARY   My, what epaulets!

They rush away in a dance.

OLD PRINCESS (*looking at the officers*)   Doubtless, the officers are all brutes. Without a brain in the bonnet. But young! So young! What a pity almost all are cripples!

Werner approaches.

OLD PRINCESS   Do you not dance, doctor?

WERNER (*pretending*)   No, I've never learned how.

OLD PRINCESS   I adore dancing! How I love the balls in Moscow. Especially when it's freezing! The glittering hall, the bared shoulders, the uniforms with their epaulets. I love it when a blizzard rages outside while inside the chandeliers and the candles are blazing, and the scent of orchids is overwhelming.

WERNER   And all the while, some pitiful orphan is freezing to death right beside the entrance way.

OLD PRINCESS   You're a sour man, doctor! And that Pechorin is just plain jaundiced! And yet, he's so handsome! Look at the dancers—how they spin and twirl! The music goes faster and faster.

WERNER   Allow me to take your pulse. (*Feeling her pulse.*) Tomorrow, I will administer leeches.

OLD PRINCESS   Very well. But doctor! Help my daughter, my little Mary.

Pechorin: In Memoriam ⌐

WERNER   I am all attention, Princess!

OLD PRINCESS   She is completely indifferent to men.

WERNER   Well? The Princess is a well-behaved young lady!

OLD PRINCESS   It's unnatural! And what does "a softened brain" mean? (*Speaking English.*)

WERNER (*after a pause*)   I'm not good at English. I could prescribe her some sulf—

OLD PRINCESS   No, not that!

WERNER   Well, then I'll let her blood too.

OLD PRINCESS   Excellent! Doctor! Only don't just stand there!

WERNER   What would you like me to do?

OLD PRINCESS   Carry me away, into this wild spinning music!

WERNER   I'll try! Off we go!!!

They speed away in a dance.

***

Pechorin, Vera

VERA   Is she pretty? Tell me, do you find her pretty? I know she's adorable, I know. It's all over with me. You keep looking at her. Oh, I know you! She catches your eye. Oh, I can see it. She feels your charismatic charm. You'll ruin me! You'll ruin us all! Here comes my husband. Please, don't stare at him like that! Look away! Oh, he's fallen down. He's very old, you know. Don't go over. Someone else will help him up. The Dragoons are helping him, even without limbs of their own. Doctor Werner is twirling around. This dancing doctor, he is very strange…. Ah, Mary! She's a sweet child! How she looks at you with her black eyes.

PECHORIN   He's not that old. As it turns out, he's not very old at all.

VERA   Why have you turned pale?

PECHORIN   Why do you refuse to meet me, Vera?

VERA   You've grown very pale. Why have you grown so pale?

PECHORIN   Are you refusing me a secret tryst, Vera?

VERA   There's sweat on your brow.

PECHORIN   My collar is too stiff. This may be our last meeting, Vera. Give me a chance to see you again. One last time. Please, I beg you. Life may part us forever this time.

VERA   It's not clear at all which of us is going to die first, it's not clear yet!

PECHORIN   Vera, I'm bored! I'm so bored, Vera!

VERA   What's happening to the music? This isn't music—it's a tornado!

PECHORIN   Let's take a spin!

> *They speed away in a dance. Vera is convulsed by a coughing fit. The music keeps up. The wounded officers, the old people of the spa society, the ladies from the Russian steppes, and the elegant young ladies with elaborate hairdos are all dancing; Doctor Werner dexterously spins his lady and pairs her up with Vera's husband; then he spits, leaps out of the vortex, and stops on the sidelines, resting. He drinks with the crippled Dragoons who are unable to dance. Pechorin has also switched partners. Vera is dancing with Grushnitsky; Pechorin with Mary.*

Pechorin: In Memoriam

***

Pechorin, Mary, later Grushnitsky

PECHORIN   Princess, how do you like Grushnitsky's uniform?

MARY (*after a pause*)   I thought you two were friends.

PECHORIN   You are prejudiced against me.

MARY   Not at all.

PECHORIN   Completely prejudiced!

MARY   I just told you, not at all!

PECHORIN   Grushnitsky is a cadet!

MARY   He is? I thought that....

PECHORIN   What is it you thought?

MARY   Nothing.

PECHORIN   Did you think he was cashiered for a duel?

MARY   I still find Grushnitsky very interesting.

PECHORIN   He's been awarded the St. George's Cross. It's the highest award for courage in action, more valuable than silver and gold.

MARY   So— you are capable of speaking well of others.

PECHORIN   Of anyone, if merited. Grushnitsky is brave in battle. He rushes forward, closing his eyes and brandishing his sword.... This is not Russian courage somehow.

MARY   My aunt looks so sad.

PECHORIN   Your aunt?

MARY   Vera. She seems sad beyond words. Why are looking at me like that?

PECHORIN   You are extremely beautiful. Beauty has always attracted me.

MARY   There are legends about you. They say you are fatal. They say you ruin women!

PECHORIN   Nobody loves women as I do. Nobody knows them as I do. Trust me, Princess, I know what love is.

MARY   What is it then?

PECHORIN   May God spare you it, Princess.

Grushnitsky approaches.

My friend Grushnitsky!

GRUSHNITSKY (*with a bow*)   Princess! Pechorin!

PECHORIN   Werner was mistaken.

GRUSHNITSKY   How so?

PECHORIN   He said that this coat brings you under the general rule. On the contrary, it makes you look even younger. A regular cherub. Am I right, Princess?

MARY   You are, Pechorin.

GRUSHNITSKY   You've won your wager—though not quite.

He joins the group of Dragoons, and exchanges whispers
with the Captain.
The latter heads toward the Princess and Pechorin.

MARY (*to Pechorin*)   You're a bizarre person!

PECHORIN   I am a wretched person, Princess.

MARY   So you can feel?

PECHORIN   Do you believe I can't?

Pechorin: In Memoriam

CAPTAIN   Princess, if I may ... I'm drunk, but so what—I can still ... I claim you for the mazurka, Princess!

MARY   Help me!

PECHORIN   Leave her alone, sir!

CAPTAIN   Watch out, you Petersburg dandy!

MARY (*to Pechorin*)   Get me away! Please, get me away from him!

VERA (*as she dances by*)   As for the tryst, yes, I will! You're skating on thin ice, as always, Pechorin. But I will. If you want to meet in secret, so be it! Oh, how quickly we burn out! Some will die sooner, others—later!

MARY   Give me your hand!

PECHORIN   Off we go!

> *They throw themselves into the dance. The ranks of the dancers are in disarray: strange, dangerous looking, dark people are flashing by in their midst. Screams are heard: "Chechens! Chechens! Oh, God, Chechens!" The dance transforms into a wild lezginka. The Old Princess and Vera's husband are livelier than the rest.*
>
> *The dark people—shadows with silky, fluid movements—start disappearing imperceptibly. Up high, above the ball, a cage is seen floating. In the cage sits Kazbich. Kazbich sees Pechorin and starts shouting.*

KAZBICH   Hey, you, are you a savage? A bonehead? I'll kill you. Give me back my horse. Hey, you—a dimwit, a child? I will kill you! Give me back my horse! Listen, I will kill you—give me back my horse! Take my hat, if you want! Listen, I will kill you, give me back my horse. Take my burka if you like. Listen, I'll kill you, give me back my horse. Take my dagger if

91

you want. Such a dagger, a Turkish one! I'll kill you, kill you, give my horse back to me! My horse is a devil, give him back to me. You're cultured, you're from Petersburg, what do you need him for? Oh, my horse, my horse, my Karagyoz, he has such warm nostrils, he loves salt! You dog, you infidel, he'll never take salt from you! Ah, my horse, my wicked horse, with legs like strings, with hooves like little coins, perfect for leaping over the treacherous stones. On your steppes he will break his legs! Listen, I'll kill you, kill you—give my horse back! Take Bela, if you like. Take Bela, you dog, but give me my horse. I'm going to kill you anyway....

Below he cannot be heard.

Pechorin: In Memoriam

ACT II

Scene 1: Magician's performance.

The entire "spa society" in attendance. A magician is performing tricks (he pulls a rabbit, doves, handkerchiefs from a top hat, from his mouth come balloons, flowers, etc). Applause.

OLD PRINCESS   It's so hot! Wake up, Vera! This is none other than Alfelbaum!

VERA   Is he still swallowing swords?

The magician spits fire.

OLD PRINCESS   No, he's spitting fire. We have sulfuric vapors here.

VERA   It's so chilly! Where is Mary?

CAPTAIN OF DRAGOONS (*in another group*)   Eh, I wish I had that gift! Let me tell you, spitting fire is not like driving rebels over the mountains!

OLD PRINCESS   The dragoons are drunk. Are they ever sober?

VERA   Where is Mary? Mary?

OLD PRINCESS   Vera, please stop fidgeting and see to your husband. It's unbearably hot! Is he spitting fire to make things worse?

VERA   Where's Mary? Ah, there she is!

OLD PRINCESS   My dear! Mary doesn't have whiskers and wear a sheepskin coat! That's Pechorin.

93

VERA   Is it?

OLD PRINCESS   I will marry him to Mary.

Vera faints.

Water!

The magician spits a water-fountain.

CAPTAIN OF DRAGOONS   Grushnitsky, this magician is a wonder! What a man! Nothing weak-kneed about him, not like some others around here.

GRUSHNITSKY   Stop it, everyone can hear!

CAPTAIN OF DRAGOONS   God dammit! One-two! (*Spits.*)

The Dragoons are whooping it up.

OLD PRINCESS   Someone, make that ruffian quiet.

Pechorin escorts the Captain out.

Vera, come to your senses, Pechorin has taken the Captain out!

VERA   Mary, Mary! Where is she?

OLD PRINCESS   What do you mean, where? She's been sitting behind you the entire time.

VERA   Oh, my little Mary!

MARY   Auntie, I'm going to marry that man, time permitting.

Vera faints again.

OLD PRINCESS   Fie, how they've smoked up this place!

Applause.

MAGICIAN   And now, ladies and gentlemen, a special act, prepared exclusively for you. You will be surprised at the lifelike appearance of the participants. You will find their speech impressively clear and convincing. You will think that they are actually present, in the room with you, but you will be mistaken. No matter how ardently you desire it, no matter now much you long for their presence, they will never be with you. They will be anywhere but here, on the summit of Mount Elbrus, say, but not here, not with you. They will merely allow you to gaze at their simulacra, you must be content with that. And now ... abracadabra, appear!

> *He throws back the left lapel of his cape; the Demon[3] jumps out. The Demon's acrobatic dance. The magician throws back the right lapel of his cape; out jumps Tamara in a golden halter and loose-fitting pants. Her dance.*

DEMON   I am the Demon!

TAMARA   I am Tamara!

> *A circus routine. The text of the Demon is heard. The small theater fills with smoke.*
> *Mary, Vera, Pechorin.*

VERA   What do you mean by "time permitting"?

MARY   Auntie, I'm younger than you. I'm practically a girl still. My poor, dear Vera, how your cheeks are burning!

VERA   What do you mean, what do you mean by "time permitting"?

MARY   Look how adorable they are. They look so lifelike.

---

[3]   Both Demon and Tamara are characters from Lermontov's famous poem *Demon* (completed in 1839), which Sadur mentions a few lines later.

VERA   It's all hocus-pocus. Visual illusion.

MARY   I saw Elbrus through a spyglass once. Over there, they look completely different, of course.

VERA   Oh, don't torture me, Mary, don't torture me! Tell me, what you mean by "time permitting"? Do you know something I don't?

MARY   I'll have to marry, sooner or later. Such is a woman's destiny.

VERA   Yes, of course! You're incredibly pretty, you're wealthy, you'll find yourself a lot of eligible suitors.

MARY   Without a doubt.

VERA   Then why "time permitting"?

MARY   Because this is Pechorin we are talking about.

VERA   Oh yes! He's one of a kind! If you only knew!

MARY   Vera, he does with us as he likes.

VERA   But that's what's so intoxicating!

MARY   Yes! Like a fast-tempo waltz!

VERA   Like a waltz over the abyss!

MARY   Caution abandoned in his faithless embrace.

VERA   And still, one would give everything—absolutely every-thing—for a single one of those languid, penetrating glances!

MARY   And for that small, wicked mouth.

VERA   Oh, how unhappy he is!

MARY   And for those blond curls!

VERA   Yes! Yes!

MARY   His kisses must be moist and soft.

Pechorin: In Memoriam

VERA   Why would you think that?

MARY   It's just an impression.

VERA   No, no, they are more like bites. He has referred to himself as a vampire.

MARY (*unsteady*)   I'm not well!

PECHORIN (*who has been eavesdropping, leads her off into the magician's cape*)   Hurry, hurry, to Alfelbaum! Look up, don't be afraid, I'm with you.

MARY   What are you doing to me? Good God! (*They kiss.*)

PECHORIN   There are moments when I understand the vampire.

Erotic scene.

MARY   Do you despise me, or love me very much? Perhaps you want to laugh at me? And then leave me. But that's base, unthinkable. Surely, there's nothing in me to prevent respect.... Answer, speak, let me hear your voice.... Perhaps you wish me to be first to say I love you?

PECHORIN   What would that prove?

MARY   Your face is sallow. Are you ill?

PECHORIN   I didn't sleep last night.

MARY   Nor did I. I tried to justify you to myself. I beg you, tell me what you're thinking.

PECHORIN   Everything?

MARY   Everything.... Only tell me the truth, and hurry. Are you afraid my family will object? It doesn't matter. I know how to sacrifice when I love. Oh, answer quickly and have pity. You don't despise me, do you?

Nina Sadur

PECHORIN   I shall tell you the whole truth, Princess. I shall neither defend myself nor explain my actions. I do not love you.

MARY   Leave me. (*Runs off.*)

Vera appears.

VERA   Yes, yes, yes, this instant! A secret tryst!

Pechorin takes her into the magician's cape. An erotic scene.

Now do you believe I love you? Oh, for a long time I wavered, for a long time I was tormented, but you can do with me as you like.

PECHORIN   Vera, in all this world I love only you. What proof do you need?

VERA   You aren't going to marry Mary? You don't love her? And she thinks ... do you know, she is madly in love with you, poor thing!

PECHORIN   Vera, you're the only person I have never been able to deceive. Yes, I do love you, I am prepared to die for you. But Vera, my heart has long grown cold.

Both leave. Mary. Vera.

MARY   Vera, let me whisper something in your ear. (*Whispers to her.*)

VERA   But how could we do it?

Mary whispers again.

I'd heard about the duel, but how can we be present? Women aren't allowed. They can only serve as the pretext. How are we going to join a half-drunken gang of officers? And climb the cliffs! We'll fall over the side! Why does everyone torment me? Every single person.

MARY Vera, darling, your cheeks are burning, your lips are feverish, and it hurts me to see you this way. My darling, sweet aunt, a woman's prime is brief; we'll wither away and only be remembered for a birthmark, or lusterless, velvety eyes. In the meantime, all they can say is, "Tomorrow I'll die!" At the balls and parties they only whine about death. But still, they have it better! Please, let's do it, Verochka, my dear Verochka. He's such a handsome fellow, let's help him! He'll only thank us. Oh— they're fighting already!

> *There is a melee in the company of Dragoons.*
>
> *Grushnitsky, Dragoons, Captain, Pechorin.*

GRUSHNITSKY (*to the Captain*) You don't believe me? I heard every word with my own two ears: using the magician as cover, she said to Pechorin "A secret tryst!" Not a minute ago.

CAPTAIN And what about him?

GRUSHNITSKY And he—as if you don't know, Pechorin—oh, "I love you, but my heart has grown cold!" How do you like the Princess's behavior, eh? That Moscow prude?

PECHORIN You've gone too far, my friend. Not only have you acted like a complete scoundrel, you've told a scurrilous lie!

PECHORIN This means a duel!

GRUSHNITSKY (*to Pechorin*) Whenever you like!

PECHORIN Good!

MARY Aha!

VERA Aha! (*They embrace.*)

Scene 2: Full moon.

The gallery with the wells, vapors, the grapevines growing over its lusterless glass. In a different spot, Grushnitsky, the Captain. Pechorin has hidden inside the Ermolov bath.

CAPTAIN   Oh, come, Grushnitsky, we won't put balls into one of the pistols at all.

GRUSHNITSKY   That's base!

CAPTAIN   It's just a joke. I swear to God, just looking at him makes me sick. He's gallivanting around Petersburg, while our mothers are counting chickens in their tiny, shabby houses in the steppes.

GRUSHNITSKY   We're noblemen, too!

CAPTAIN   Eh, brother, before a Chechen bullet we are all nobility, but for the rest of the world you are an insignificant beggar while he is a beaver-clad blueblood. It's not like we're planning to kill him. We'll just give His Haughtiness a good scare. Just like that: poof, and he'll wet his pants!

MARY   He won't come out alive! (*Mary hugs Vera.*)

GRUSHNITSKY   I heard a squeal!

CAPTAIN   It was just a vine rubbing against glass. There's always a draft in these galleries.

GRUSHNITSKY   Fine, fine, but only give me your word that there will be no murder....

CAPTAIN   A nobleman's word!

GRUSHNITSKY   To be honest, he has wronged me, too. And I used to love him like a brother.

Pechorin: In Memoriam

PECHORIN (*from inside the bath*)   Scoundrel!

CAPTAIN   What was that?

GRUSHNITSKY   Muck. Nonsense. The sound of sulfuric bubbles bursting.

CAPTAIN   We have to hurry: we need to find a doctor.

GRUSHNITSKY   Anything that will make it easier.

CAPTAIN   I called on two yesterday, and their avarice was maddening. They started out speaking of duty and ended with demands for an advance. I couldn't let such mercenaries have anything to do with the duel.

GRUSHNITSKY   I know a crazy doctor. You can get him straight out of bed; he'll start getting ready at the mere word "duel," and he charges no money at all!

CAPTAIN   That does honor to humanity and to the medical calling. Have you found a carriage?

GRUSHNITSKY   Not yet, to be honest.

CAPTAIN   There's still time. We need a carriage for four; it's impossible to tend a wounded man or transport a dead one in a brougham.

GRUSHNITSKY   A dead one? But you said....

CAPTAIN   The rules must be observed; and don't eat beforehand. A bullet can slide in and fly out without damage to the intestines if they retain their elasticity.

GRUSHNITSKY   I only take coffee in the morning.

CAPTAIN   It's settled then. Let's go, there's still much to do. (*They leave.*)

Vera. Mary.

MARY   Bonjour, Captain. Is everything ready?

VERA   I've brought two sets of pistols pairs with me, the finest.[4]

MARY   Have you tested the bullets?

VERA   The bullets were manufactured in Paris for special accuracy. They're in good working order.

MARY   I wouldn't count on it, Captain. I once made a fool of myself by not checking. I still blush when I recall the incident: the second round got stuck in the barrel, and try as we might, we couldn't push them into place. The parties had no choice but to use saddle pistols. Fortunately, one of them got the other right in the forehead, where any bullet, be it smaller than a pea or larger than a cherry, has the same effect.

VERA   Fortunate, indeed.

MARY   But imagine what reproaches if the shots had shattered an arm or a leg?

VERA   Isn't that's the truth!

MARY   Is your gunpowder polished?

VERA   Yes, and fine-grained.

MARY   So much the worse. Forget it. Let's just use regular rifle gunpowder. Polished powder doesn't always catch as quickly. See for yourself. (*A flash.*) Sometimes the spark doesn't catch at all.

VERA   What are we going to do about the fast-firing mechanisms?

---

[4] In the text, Kuchenreuters and Lepages. Nineteenth-century German and French percussion pistols, respectively, both popularly used in duels.

Pechorin: In Memoriam

MARY   Yes! Yes! Those damned things always interfere with the aim; thanks to them many a good man has been killed. It's practically impossible to avoid engaging the mechanism; the slightest movement of the finger can turn it on! These gun-makers are such rascals—they seem to think pistols were invented solely to be used in shooting clubs.

VERA   Wouldn't it be better to outlaw their use altogether? What are your thoughts, Your Eminence?

MARY   I'd give it unqualified support. Well now, are the bullets ready?

VERA   How lucky we are that the moon will be full tonight. Our bullets are impeccable! (*They leave.*)

Pechorin slips as he climbs out of the bath.
The Doctor enters.

PECHORIN   Lend me your hand, Doctor!

Doctor helps the freezing Pechorin out of the bath.

(*His teeth chattering from the cold*). Doctor, you've been called a madman.

WERNER   But I never prescribed night-time baths. Sulfuric steam, especially when combined with moonlight, can produce highly adverse results.

PECHORIN   There's to be a duel; you've been engaged already.

WERNER   There's going to be a *what*?!

PECHORIN   Do you know that the mountain people are petrified of these sulfur springs? They call them the devil's urine.

WERNER   And whom will you be fighting?

PECHORIN   The adorable Muscovite Princess!

WERNER   My God!

PECHORIN   And, alas, Vera!

WERNER   And, alas, Vera?!

PECHORIN   Don't worry, Grushnitsky is going to be there as well.

WERNER   I'm not worried. Is this your handiwork?

PECHORIN   Perhaps. Doctor, you must be my second.

WERNER   I'll not stand for murder. Especially when ladies are present....

PECHORIN   You're going to be hired anyhow. They'll need a medic to extract the bullet, etcetera.

WERNER   I loathe duels!

PECHORIN   You'll do it then?

WERNER   Here's my hand.

The duel. A steep cliff over the precipice.

CAPTAIN   Toss the coin.

Werner takes a coin out of his pocket and throws it.

GRUSHNITSKY   Tails!

PECHORIN   Heads.

The coin falls.

You're lucky. Tails.

WERNER (*to Pechorin*)   It's time....

PECHORIN   Not a word, doctor!

Pechorin: In Memoriam ᔧ

WERNER   All right then, if this is what you want! Only don't bring complaints against me in the next world.

CAPTAIN (*whispers to Grushnitsky*)   Nature is a ninny, fate is a henny, and life is a penny!

> *Pechorin stands on the very edge of the precipice.*
>
> *Grushnitsky, having counted out the steps, takes aim.*

GRUSHNITSKY   I can't.

CAPTAIN   Coward!

> *Grushnitsky fires a shot, Pechorin stumbles, but limps forward*
> *and avoids falling into the abyss.*

CAPTAIN   Well, brother Grushnitsky, now it's your turn, take your stand.

> *Grushnitsky walks to the edge of precipice;*
> *Pechorin doesn't let him pass.*

GRUSHNITSKY   Let go. It's your turn to shoot now.

PECHORIN   What would be the point? The pistol is empty.

> *Grushnitsky grabs hold of Pechorin and the two of them hover*
> *perilously over the abyss. Pechorin, with all his might,*
> *pulls Grushnitsky away from the edge.*

GRUSHNITSKY   I hate you for making me hate life!

CAPTAIN (*bellows and hops from rock to rock like a caveman*)   This is against the rules! Separate, immediately!

> *Grushnitsky and Pechorin are still wrestling.*

PECHORIN (*his nose broken*)   The mischievous wind blows,

Buyanka's barking, down the icy hill, blue sleds are sliding. The old grandpa made these sleds for his little Vanya. The old grandpa has come to watch the sleds fly.[5]

Mary and Vera rush in.

CAPTAIN   It's against the rules! (*Throws stones at them.*)

Everybody fires shots, even the Captain.
When the smoke clears, nobody is left.

MARY   Are they both gone? But I was shooting at Pechorin.

VERA   So was I!

MARY   Then I was the one who killed him?

VERA   Why you?

In the meantime the Captain has crawled to the edge of the abyss;
he roars.

CAPTAIN   There's only one here!

MARY AND VERA   Who is it?

CAPTAIN   Grushnitsky. Your man is not there. He's gone.

WERNER   Allow me. (*Looks into the abyss; Mary looks with him.*)

MARY (*to Werner*)   Death is obscene.

WERNER   I know, Princess!

CAPTAIN   Where has the other one gone?

VERA   Oh, yes! Now I remember! As I was taking aim at him, a dark bird with sharp talons swooped in and carried him off.

CAPTAIN   You're lying, madam! The other one has escaped!

---

[5]   A slightly misquoted excerpt from a Russian children's ditty.

Pechorin: In Memoriam

VERA No, I'm not lying. I read about these birds in a book I found in my father's study when I was a child. These are prehistoric creatures with teeth, wings, and webbed talons. He was carried off by a bird like that. I saw it!

MARY Doctor, what's more revolting, death or lust?

WERNER That's a mathematical riddle, Princess.

Vera's husband crawls in.

VERA'S HUSBAND Vera! Be strong! I'm here! (*Shoots.*)

VERA He's been killed! Killed! A dark bird has carried him off!

VERA'S HUSBAND What horror! Who's been killed?

VERA Pechorin! You should know this then! I love him! I've always loved him. I'm ruined, but I don't care anymore. I've always been his lover, even before I knew you. There was no one, no one at all, just the two of us. And if you must know— I followed him here!

VERA'S HUSBAND Whore! You'll get nothing! I'll kick you out! Barefoot in the snow! And your boy too will end up barefoot in the snow ... instead of the lyceum! And somebody will put a piece of bread in his little hand. Phew, what the devil...! "Instead of bread they put into his begging hand ..." I forgot what.... You're a whore.

DOCTOR You need to get back to bed at once. You must have some hot milk and go to bed. (*Addressing the rest of the group.*) I'll talk to you later.

VERA'S HUSBAND What did they put in his cold little hand? I forget.

VERA   A stone.

VERA'S HUSBAND   Villains! Such a cruel, heartless world! They put a stone into the outstretched hand of a little child! (*He's carried off.*)

Captain weeps.

MARY   Vera, we did everything right. His body must have rolled out of sight.

VERA   You weren't quick enough. He didn't die. He was carried off by that prehistoric bird from my father's book. I saw it!

Pechorin: In Memoriam ⟿

EPILOGUE

A mountain trail.

M.M., Bela, Kazbich, Pechorin.

Later, below, the spa society.

M.M.   Eh, Grigory Aleksandrovich, I knew you'd be back.

PECHORIN   Why is that? However, I must admit, it's as thrilling now as it was then. Are we on the same trail?

M.M.   No, a different one. I'm taking you to see a splendid view, my brother! Such luminosity! Would you believe it, even I, seasoned old man that I am, fall to my knees every time I see it.

PECHORIN   What is it, Maksim Maksimych?

M.M.   In these parts, a caprice of nature creates a light on Elbrus when the sun battles the snow and the two meet in competition with the entire sky! Eh, I don't know how to describe it, I'm sorry!

PECHORIN   On the contrary, your description is very picturesque. Are we going to get there on time?

M.M.   Judging by the signs, we are. We can stop pushing the horses. See—there they are!

PECHORIN   What?

M.M.   The Caucasus, I'm saying.

PECHORIN   Very pretty.

M.M.   I kept waiting and thinking we were going to see each other again, Grigory Aleksandrovich.

PECHORIN   Why so certain?

M.M.   What do you mean? After all, you and I are old friends. That's something that can't be wiped out. Yes, brother, wherever Pechorin goes, Maksim Maksimych goes too.

PECHORIN   I'm touched, dear Maksim Maksimych. I, too, remember you warmly. What's this?

Up ahead, a glittering tent appears in sight.

M.M.   We've gotten lost. This isn't the way. Mercy on us, Grigory Aleksandrovich. This is where the savages live, let's just forget about it!

PECHORIN (*enters the tent*)   Hello, my lovely!

BELA (*over his shoulder*)   Hello, Maksim Maksimych!

M.M.   Eh, Bela, my child, hello, my dove!

BELA   Have you brought an infidel with you?

M.M.   A guest, an old companion.

PECHORIN   Pechorin.

BELA   Pechorin.

M.M.   We must have gotten lost. Sorry, my girl. Grigory Aleksandrovich, she is a complete child, and I—would you believe it—I don't even have children of my own.

PECHORIN   What wild, ineffable beauty.

M.M.   We should be on our way; otherwise we're going to miss the light over Elbrus.

PECHORIN   Peri.[6] Are you a peri?

---

[6]   A word of Persian origin widely used in many of the Northern Caucasian languages, a rough equivalent of "fairy" in English.

Pechorin: In Memoriam

BELA (*lighting a hookah*)   Try it, Infidel. Pechorin.

M.M.   Don't trust her, brother Pechorin. Bela is a kind girl, but this is the Caucasus.

Pechorin takes a puff on the hookah.

I don't smoke such stuff. Bring me a piece of melon and a juicy fig, my girl. Eh, this man always gets into trouble, and in such a restive spot!

BELA (*showing a toy horse*)   See what I have. I was sad, so Maksim Maksimych carved me a little horse out of wood, as if I were a baby still.

M.M.   Don't embarrass me, Bela! You always were a mischief-maker.

PECHORIN   Let me see that…. (*Studies the toy.*) This is Karagyoz, the spitting image! M.M., whatever happened to that beggar— Kazbich, wasn't it?

M.M.   He vanished.

PECHORIN   Poor thing.

M.M.   Ever since Karagyoz perished, sir, he's vanished.

PECHORIN   How did you know that Karagyoz perished?

M.M.   I don't know how I knew. But this is the Caucasus, sir.

PECHORIN   You're right; Karagyoz didn't make it in our lowlands and broke his leg. I had to shoot him. Dammit, I really regret it, Maksim Maksimych.

M.M.   You didn't intend harm, did you, Grigory Aleksandrovich? You simply craved beauty.

PECHORIN   But I did. What if I did intend harm? And rode the horse to his death out of spite?

M.M.   Such a horse is impossible not to love, sir. You know that!

PECHORIN   I do. Dance, Bela!

M.M.   Bela is a superb dancer. She has often danced for me, me, an old man; she's a kind girl.

BELA   Handsome Infidel, Pechorin, do you like my little horse?

PECHORIN   I like *you*, my heart. But why are you trying to slip away, Bela?

M.M.   Grigory Ivanych, I implore you, for the sake of our old friendship, leave her alone. She's just a wild girl. And a child.

PECHORIN   Tell me, Bela, you're not in love with some Chechen, are you?

BELA   Yokh.[7]

PECHORIN   Or with a rich Circassian prince?

BELA: Yokh.

PECHORIN   Then why don't you love me, my girl?

BELA   You are an infidel, Pechorin.

PECHORIN   There is one God. He has taught us to love. But you're slipping away, and I can't even touch you.

M.M.   It's the hookah, sir, the most treacherous of all things.

PECHORIN   Eh, no, Bela, you're treacherous, you'd break my poor heart.

BELA   I want to love your poor heart. Shall I dance for you?

---

[7]   Yokh, in Turkish and a number of Turkic languages, means no.

M.M.   That's something she knows how to do! Dance, my child, joy of my life!

Bella dances. They are high from smoking the hookah.

PECHORIN   Or do you, gentlemen, think that I rejoice in my indifference, that I revel in the suffering of others? Every person I put in his grave is a person I mourn. It's true, my tears are spiteful, but I've no other kind. Outwardly, I'm young, handsome, and strong, but inwardly, I'm an old man, and my heart, which wants love, is eaten by malice.

BELA   My little horse, I'll kiss his warm nostrils and give him salt. (*Rocking the horse.*) Infidel Pechorin, I've seen your face before; I saw it floating over the abyss. I wept. But I knew you would come and fall in love with your *Janechka*.[8] I can dance for a long, long time and not get winded at all!

M.M.   She pined a lot, sir, so I made this horse for her. She plays with it as if it were a doll. She's really a child. She's never met a man like you. You can't imagine how easy it is for you to ruin her!

PECHORIN   Since we're not going to make it to Elbrus, I might just as well spend the rest of my days here—as if in Eden. A man can't pass his whole life wandering about feeling sad. If you detest an everyday peaceful existence, all you have to do is come here, to this mysterious place among the cliffs and gorges, to feel at one with them and let your spirit soar. God will find a corner even for a mutinous soul like mine. I love you, my Bela!

---

[8]   As Maksim Maksimych explains in *Hero of Our Time*, the equivalent of "darling."

Kazbich enters and sees Bela's horse.

KAZBICH   Give me my horse!

*Stabs Bela in the back, wrestles the horse out of her hands, kisses
and caresses it, cries over it. Pechorin, high from the hookah,
"floats," trying to catch Kazbich. The latter throws him off with
a kick and continues to pace about, mourning his horse.*

M.M. (*rocking Bella*)   In the back, the most treacherous blow!
Savage!

*The tent is gone. A trail. Pechorin walks on it. Up above, an
unimaginable clash of lights—snow, sun, and sky—appears: it is
Elbrus lighting up. Pechorin trudges upward toward the spectacle.
On the edge of the trail sits M.M., his bare feet hanging over the
edge. Far below them is the spa society. Everyone is animated,
some dancing, some looking at Elbrus through a telescope, some
taking the waters; Werner is checking pulses and tongues.*

M.M.   What a blizzard! How you blow, as if this were not the
Caucasus but the steppe, the boundless Russian steppe. You
must have swallowed up the abyss and salved every wound.
Blow, my love, blow merry and merrier, my beloved!

The spa society in a blizzard.

CURTAIN

January 19, 1999
Peredelkino

Translated from the Russian
by ***Margarit T. Ordukhanyan***

RED PARADISE

A Play in One Act

CHARACTERS

TAISA (TAISKA, TAISA ALANOVNA):
a homeless woman of uncertain age

VOLODYA (VOVA)
and TOLYA (TOLIK, ANATOLY):
two young men

MAN WITH A DONKEY

The action takes place in the town of Sudak and in the Genovese fortress at Soldaiya.

TAISA (*sings*) "The planes fly from afar, the darkness stretches below. The waves rise high, the riddle is lost in the trough. Now it's calm on the sea, on the blue; the engines and pilots are gone. The water is oily grey, but the sky is insanely blue. They looked for them long and hard, but they couldn't be found at all. The riddle was silent, the riddle is silent—now and forever, now and forever."

VOLODYA Shut up!

TAISA No, I won't. (*Sings.*) "I am the earth, seeing my children off—daughters and sons. Fly to the sun and come home soon!"

VOLODYA I'll pull your teeth out in a minute, then you'll forget how to screech.

TAISA Quiet! (*Sings.*) "Lavender, proud lavender. The passionate love of our rendezvous!"

VOLODYA Pig! To mess up a song like that!

Taisa cries, then howls.

TAISA I don't like *your* songs.

VOLODYA Then don't sing.

TAISA I will sing.

VOLODYA   Why don't you leave? The dogs will come running and tear you to bits.

TAISA (*sings*)   "The dogs will come running and tear me to bits." There's another song! You don't know any songs.

VOLODYA   I'm going to crack your head open. Come closer, it's too hot to get up.

TAISA   Did you see? Did you? They tore down the little house on Commune Street. They put a seal on the door, wrote something down, the house went boom, bang, and they smashed it to bits. Everybody voted, hooray! They stomped their feet, bang, boom, broke everything up. The house started to tremble … and then collapsed. Everyone votes: Hooray! Hooray! The pebbles rolled away. The little red pebbles, blood dripping from one of them. You bet. The house cried and cried, and a grandma jumped out and started running. It fell down and everyone clapped. They put up a flag. The grandma rushed to the bazaar and hid herself under a board. She's selling lady fingers now, two-fifty a kilo.

VOLODYA   If I felt like getting up, I'd pluck your eyes out.

TAISA   It's illegal! Illegal! The fine is three rubles!

VOLODYA   I'd pay for the pleasure.

TAISA   Right. But watch out. There's a serious danger of fire in our town—crackle, crackle….

VOLODYA (*looking up*)   What's that? A helicopter or what?

TAISA   It's flying! It's just hanging up there in the sky and doesn't fall down! And it's made of iron! Highly illegal!

VOLODYA   Now I'm really getting mad. When I get up I'm going to rip you to shreds.

Tolya enters.

Tolya, get her over here so I can strangle her.

TOLYA (*to Taisa*) Do you know how little kittens die? They go off somewhere, and no one sees them die. Baby elephants and puppies and mice die like that, too.

VOLODYA She'd better tell me where she got that melon. Huh? Where did you get the melon? Did you swipe it?

TAISA Hands up!

TOLYA She hasn't forgotten the time you went after her. When you chased her in the truck? Adka was there too.

VOLODYA Ha, ha! Too bad I didn't run her over. What do you think—would we get nabbed for running over a retard?

TOLYA We would.

VOLODYA Too bad. I'm sick of her. The minute I see her, I feel like shit.

TAISA Attention! Young man, can you give me a cigarette?

VOLODYA I'll give you a pitchfork in the teeth.

TAISA You can't.

TOLYA (*to Taisa*) Taisa, just leave, you must see how worked up Vova's getting. He'll give you a beating and then you'll start crying.

A man walks by with his donkey.

VOLODYA Oh, look who's coming now. His face is ugly, but he's rich, a millionaire. Tolya, how many millionaires do we have in Sudak?

TOLYA   Seven.

VOLODYA   You're shitting me—where do you get seven?

TOLYA   Count 'em. We have three in Uyutny and four in Dachny. And then there's the guard at the cemetery.

VOLODYA   He doesn't have a million.

TOLYA   He doesn't have a million because he's new. But his mattress is stuffed with money. You remember when we had the flood? He was trying to save his mattress. Almost drowned, but carried the mattress out.

VOLODYA   Yeah, I remember. Coffins were floating by, but there he was, swimming with his mattress. Good for him!

TAISA   Oh, run, run away from here!

VOLODYA   And where's the old geezer heading?

TOLYA (*to Taisa*)   Look, why don't you go to the bus station. They give out free cigarettes there. (*To Volodya.*) Did you see that sack he had?

VOLODYA   Maybe he's off to market?

TOLYA   I don't think so. The sack looked empty, and if he'd had peaches to sell, it would've been lumpy.

VOLODYA   Well, what should we do with him?

TOLYA   How much money do you think he has? He takes pictures of the vacationers with his donkey—five rubles a photo. Plus he sells milk from his goat....

VOLODYA   But the milk stinks.

TOLYA   Who cares? The tourists drink it. They think it's organic. And he also takes pictures of his monkey Aliska. He paid 70,000 rubles for that monkey, did you know that? And the monkey has paid for itself ten times over. Yes, ten times over. Plus he has five apricot trees, two plum trees, a peach tree, and two Greek walnut trees. Imagine! How much money do you think that adds up to?

VOLODYA   Why imagine? Just to make myself miserable?

TAISA (*from the shelter where she's hidden herself*)   Dig! Dig!

VOLODYA   He's buried his treasure!

TOLYA   I knew it the moment I saw his sack. It must be full of money.

VOLODYA   He's buried it. People always bury treasures around here.

TOLYA   Maybe he went to the bank?

VOLODYA   Oh, no! Not to the bank! No way he'd trust the bank. Here people trust only the earth. When the Scythians were here, they buried their treasure. Ossetians, too, they were here first. Trade routes all over—the Turks, the Tatars, the Byzantines, the Genovese.

TOLYA   Where did you pick that up?

VOLODYA   I read it in a book. When I was a kid.

TOLYA   You're lying again. You're illiterate.

VOLODYA   So how do I sign for my pay check?

TOLYA   All the same, there were no Ossetians here. Not then.

VOLODYA   The earth is crammed with buried treasure.

TOLYA   Where should we dig? Do you know?

TAISA   I know!

TOLYA   Where?

TAISA (*pointing*)   Over there.

VOLODYA   Just listen to the moron.

TOLYA   Where over there?

TAISA   In the Genovese fortress.

VOLODYA   You see—the idiot speaks!

TAISA (*to Volodya*)   You stay here. You're too skinny, I like guys who are more solid. Tolik, let's go to the fortress.

VOLODYA   I'll break your arm for that!

TOLYA   Wait a minute, Vova. Maybe she really does know. She goes everywhere, you know.

TAISA   I know!

VOLODYA   All right, come on out. Even though you said I'm skinny, I forgive you for now.

> *Taisa comes out of the shelter.*

TAISA   You promise you forgive me?

VOLODYA   Ooooh, you're gonna get it!

TAISA   Not allowed!

TOLYA   Leave her alone. (*To Taisa.*) Where shall we dig? Where? In the fortress?

TAISA   Yes, the fortress.

> *They go to the fortress. At the fortress.*

VOLODYA   What fools, those Genovese. They built their fortress on a mountain top. Now you have to drag yourself to the top.

TOLYA   It's for military use. It was built like that on purpose, to make it hard to reach. That's why it's called Soldaiya.

VOLODYA   Soldaiya is what the locals used to call Sudak.

TOLYA   Soldaiya means "fortress." I know. I'm a teacher.

VOLODYA   Well, all right. But what was Sudak called?

TOLYA   Do you really care?

VOLODYA   I'd just like to know what we were called before.

TOLYA   Before us it was bad. Wild.

VOLODYA   Exactly. But why are all the doors here so low?

TOLYA   In the fourteenth century people were shorter.

VOLODYA   Midgets.

TOLYA   You think *you* could build a fortress like this?

VOLODYA   What would be the point? What would we do with it? Wage war?

TOLYA   It doesn't make sense for fighting anymore, Vova. But you wouldn't be able to build a fortress like it.

VOLODYA   So what if I couldn't.

TOLYA   I wouldn't brag about that.

VOLODYA   I'm not bragging. I just don't give a shit. I know how to drive a car. Let the Genovese build a fortress if that's what they go in for.

TOLYA   But they're extinct.

VOLODYA   So fuck them.

TAISA   Over here! Come over here!

VOLODYA   Wow, it's pretty high up. What are we—goats? You want us to jump over the cliffs? Oh, Tolya—look at the rosehips! Let's pick them.

TOLYA   That's the last thing I need now!

VOLODYA   Why not? They're useful! They've never even been touched, and look at their size! I'll pick them for vitamins.

TOLYA   Either we pick rosehips or dig for millions! Choose!

VOLODYA   Tolya, they're special here, they're closer to the sun. Look how red they are! I've never seen rosehips so red. They shine like blood.

TOLYA   You'd better go and see where Taisa has gone.

VOLODYA   Oh, man! She's up so high, she'll fall off for sure!

TOLYA   The Genovese made the approach so steep for a reason.

VOLODYA   But how did they get up here?

TOLYA   Everything's in ruins. There used to be steps.

TAISA   Come on, come!

VOLODYA   Goats, those Genovese. They climbed to the top of the world. Listen, Tolya, what if she threw the sack into a pit somewhere?

TOLYA   Yeah, I was thinking that myself.

VOLODYA   Well, if it's been thrown into a pit, I'll break some heads. Especially the retard's. No one's gonna care, right?

TOLYA   Not if there's no body.

VOLODYA   I'll get rid of it. You think she understands what money is? Rubles, paper scraps, it's all the same to her. I'll kill her and then get rid of her. Retards are of no use to anyone. And society needs them even less. Society will only thank you if you kill a moron. Because a moron is a burden to society. She doesn't work—she just throws sacks into pits. I'll knock her head off.

Red Paradise

TOLYA   Don't get so worked up. You have to get hold of her first.

VOLODYA   I'll do it.

TOLYA   What's the hurry? Look out! This isn't a stroll on a beach.

VOLODYA   I'll hide the body over here. In that little shed.

TOLYA   That's not a shed. It's a Christian temple from the ninth century.

VOLODYA   So what. It looks cozy.

TOLYA   First it's rosehips, now it's breaking heads. What about the treasure? How are we going to find it without her?

VOLODYA   Ugh, the stinking bitch!

TOLYA   Do you think she wants to get it for us?

VOLODYA   She has to!

TAISA   Keep climbing! Come on! Hurry!

VOLODYA   What's wrong with you? Were you born yesterday? You can't go that way! The wall has crumbled. It's hanging over the sea. Let's go dig over here! Look how much space there is here!

TAISA   You have to come up here! Come on!

TOLYA   Look, she's made it to the top.

VOLODYA   Because she's a moron.

TOLYA   And we're no better?

VOLODYA   I won't go up there. Heights make me sick. I'm going to dig over here.

TOLYA   All right, go ahead. But I'm climbing up. I believe Taisa.

VOLODYA   He believes the retard. But this is the first time I've ever been up here. And I don't want us to fall and smash our bones all over the rocks.

125

TOLYA   The Genovese weren't afraid! In the fourteenth century. And now it's what century?

VOLODYA   Tolya, I know you're a teacher, no argument there, but you go tell your school children what century it is. I don't care if it's zero century, I'm not climbing up there.

TOLYA   The treasure is there.

They climb up.

VOLODYA   But if she really threw it into the pit....

TOLYA   All that money!

VOLODYA   But what if she scattered it to the winds?

TOLYA   In a sack!

VOLODYA   Are you sure? We're risking our lives, you know.

TOLYA   All that money.

VOLODYA   Oh, my God!

TOLYA   What is it? Are you slipping? Close your eyes! Don't look down.

VOLODYA   Tolya, look, she dug up the sack!

TOLYA   The sack!

VOLODYA   The sack!

TOLYA   Money! Money! Money! I know—money! Money!

VOLODYA   Tolya, stop jumping around! It gets really narrow here.

TOLYA   Money, money, money!

VOLODYA   I can't hold on. I'm going to fall off.

TOLYA   Money! Money! Sweet little money!

VOLODYA   I'm slipping….

TOLYA   Hey, you down there! We're millionaires!

VOLODYA   Hey, you rats down there! Tolya, what are you gonna buy?

TOLYA   Me? (*He laughs.*)

VOLODYA   Tell me!

TOLYA   Oh, a short trip to Bulgaria. I'll bring back a pair of shoes.

VOLODYA (*reaching the top*)   I'm going to buy a monkey. They're so funny.

TOLYA   We're rich! Do you understand, Vova? Vova! Here, let me kiss you! Wait—where are you going? Taisa, Taisa—stay where you are. Stay where you're standing right now.

VOLODYA   Throw that sack over here! We can't climb up to you.

TOLYA   Taisa, sweetheart, wait for us. (*To Volodya.*) Speak to her politely, or she'll run away with it. Taisa, honey, throw us the sack! You don't need it. That's a good girl! I'll let you have some beads.

VOLODYA   You don't need the money, retard. The government feeds you. Throw us the sack now!

Taisa goes into a tower.

VOLODYA   Son of a bitch! She's gone into the tower. We can't reach her there.

TOLYA   If you say so. I'm going, anyhow. But I get everything then.

Volodya and Tolya crawl into the tower.

VOLODYA   You couldn't dream this up. Tolik, are you alive?

TOLYA   Yeah, but I scraped my stomach, crawling in.

VOLODYA   I'm scratched all over, too. It's beyond belief what's out here. Hey, you saw those cliffs. How are we gonna get across?

TOLYA   We better forget about it. We'll have to get back down somehow, too. Just try to picture how the sea glitters from such heights.

VOLODYA   What did you say?

TOLYA   The sea. From up here. The world needs exploring, especially from heights like these.

VOLODYA   That's what *you* do. *You're* the teacher—it's your job. I'm a driver, I don't need to explore.

TOLYA (*they climb higher inside the tower*)   You're wrong. Do it for yourself, to broaden your horizons.

VOLODYA   And you—you'd climb right up and start exploring?

TOLYA   Yup.

VOLODYA   You're gonna break your balls.

TOLYA   For me, knowledge is the most precious thing there is.

VOLODYA (*on a landing*)   Let's lie down here where it's flat, 'cause I'm tired and shaking all over. Look at that fluffy rug in there. Let's crawl into this room, take a look. (*He does.*)

TOLYA   What rug?

VOLODYA   Wow, everything here is the way it used to be! Look at the funny furniture they had. Tolya, you could learn a lot here.

TOLYA   There shouldn't be anything in here.

VOLODYA   And what's this, in your opinion? A fancy bench of some kind. A little carved cabinet.

TOLYA   It should be empty. There should be only the ruins.

VOLODYA   Then why is all this stuff here?

TOLYA   I don't know.

VOLODYA   Well, I do. The Genovese left it. You yourself said they built the fortress to last.

TOLYA   There should be nothing but ruins here!

VOLODYA   Doesn't look like ruins to me! You'd better start on your research. These are antiquities. You can tell your school kids all about it later.

Tolya is shaking.

Why are you shaking? Quit it! Why don't you help yourself to some of this stuff? For your research. Take a rug, take something. I need money, but I don't need old junk. Old things are depressing.

TOLYA   Something's really wrong here. Something's wrong....

VOLODYA   How about we take a look in the cabinet?

TOLYA   No!!

VOLODYA   Why the hell not? We've wasted all this time climbing up here. (*He opens the cabinet.*) Oh, Tolya, just look at this! You're gonna die when you see it. There are saws, axes, hooks of some kind.... Ah, I understand now, they were military people and these were their weapons. Such teeny, tiny ones. God! Really tiny.

TOLYA You're lying. There can't be anything there. Nothing.
It's empty!

VOLODYA And what's this then? (*Points to a surgical clamp.*) Look
at the little ornamental knives they had. Take a look, Tolya—
they shine like new. They really knew how to make things back
then.

TOLYA Aaaaaaa!

VOLODYA Jeez, what are you shouting about? You're making me
sweat all over.

TOLYA New ones!?

VOLODYA Sure. They've lasted through the centuries. What's
all the screaming about? Look how tiny they are—they must
be for war, right? They have to be. And they won, after all. It's
unbelievable. They were so short in the fourteenth century, and
their weapons were small too. Just look at all this. Something to
think about, right? The history of mankind over the centuries.

TOLYA Put that down!

VOLODYA We could give it to a museum.

TOLYA Put it down! Don't touch it!

VOLODYA But why? You could open a museum in your school—
students could learn useful stuff about local history.

TOLYA Put it down, you asshole, put it down! (*He looks around.*)
How the hell are we going to get back down from here? How?
How did we get up in the first place? God, it's a straight drop.

VOLODYA Tolya, seriously, you're overreacting. If you don't
want to take anything, then don't. Let it rot here. Of course, it's

a shame that school kids won't be able to learn something from it. But I guess you know better. You teach them, not me.

TOLYA   We have to get the hell out of here, understand? We have to get out. How did we get here in the first place?

VOLODYA (*looks around*)   Shit, I don't really know. I guess you're right though. Well, we can take our time. Where's that scarecrow Taisa? We've got to make her give us the money—it'll be sunset soon, and then we won't be able to see our way back down. Hey, you old bitch, come on back! Come back!

TOLYA   Shut up!

VOLODYA   What's your problem, Tolya?

TOLYA   Just be quiet. Somebody over there is ... crying?

VOLODYA   Where?

TOLYA   Don't you hear it?

VOLODYA   That's just seagulls. What else could it be? The seagulls are making that noise. Their mewing is terrible. I can't stand it.

TOLYA   Ask her. *Ask her*. What's her patronymic?

VOLODYA   Whose patronymic?

TOLYA   Hers. Taisa's.

VOLODYA   That piece of trash? *Her patronymic*? You want to be polite to a retard?

TOLYA   Vova, it's us who are the retards. (*He calls out.*) Taisa ... Ivanovna, please, help us. We can't get out of here by ourselves. We're begging you on our knees.

VOLODYA (*afraid*)   Why are you talking to the dirty bitch like that? It's not right, Tolik! Here: Hey, come on out, you old biddy!

Nina Sadur

Or else I'll pull you out by your dirty hair! Where are you hiding? I can hear you, yes I can. Something's rustling nearby. So you're hiding someplace close.... And when I find you I'm going to beat the shit out of you.... It's better if you come out by yourself.... Look, Tolya—there's some kind of an alcove.

TOLYA   This is terrible! Don't go in there!

VOLODYA   Oh, come on!

> *He crawls into the alcove. An iron grating falls from above, piercing his chest.*

TOLYA   I told you!

VOLODYA   I'm dying, Tolya. I'm dying. Stabbed by the Genovese. See that my mother gets half the money.

> *He dies. Tolya throws himself against the wall. Taisa enters with the sack.*

TOLYA   I won't, I promise! I won't be bad anymore.

> *Taisa sits down on the floor, empties the sack, and counts the rubles.*

Maybe I can leave? All right, I'm off.

> *He can't leave because it's too steep.*

Taisa ... Ivanovna....

TAISA   Alanovna.

TOLYA   Taisa Alanovna. I'm shocked. I didn't know. No, that's not right, I always knew! I knew you were magnificent! Just say something, Taisa Alanovna, please.... You have a lot of coins there…. That's a good thing. A person can't get anywhere without money. A man without money is like a bird without wings. Don't you think so?

Taisa throws small coins at the gun slots of the tower.

That's right. Small change just makes your pockets heavy.

VOLODYA (*dying*)   Half the money goes to my mother. (*Dies.*)

TOLYA   It's sickening to listen to him. He's counting someone else's money! What a scumbag. The little shithead.

VOLODYA   Give it to my mother, you filthy bitch! You get everything paid for by the government, retard. You haven't worked a day in your life.

TOLYA   You're a pig! I should push that bar deeper. Seriously. Just give me a sign, Taisa Alanovna. Move your eyebrow and I'll understand. Don't even listen to this pig.

VOLODYA   Tolya, don't move it or I'll lose whatever blood I've got left.

TOLYA   Taisa Alanovna, just say the word. Where's a lever? Say the word and I'll find it.

VOLODYA   Tolya, my stomach's on fire. I have seen death and it still shines in my eyes. I'm back, but I don't know for how long. Tell that filthy whore I don't excuse her ugliness.

TOLYA   Taisa Alanovna, marry me!

VOLODYA   Oh! Tolik! (*He dies again.*)

TOLYA   We'll climb down. How do you get out of here? We're going to go down, right? Into the world? Our little town?

I have a sunny little house. I rent five beds to vacationers for two rubles fifty. I have a little garden. I'll build an addition for three more cots. There's space. Eight beds. I'll hang, they'll hang my picture … on the Hall of Fame plaque. Taisa, I've been attracted to you for a long time. I was just afraid to approach you. You are proud. Taisa, be my wife. I love you.

Taisa throws all the money at the tower's gun slots. The rubles fly around in the wind.

TOLYA   All right, then! We will be poor but happy!

TAISA   The money belongs to the people.

TOLYA   Aaaaah!!!

He throws himself off the cliff. The sound of his body is heard, hitting the rocks below.
The man who owns the donkey appears in the tower room.

MAN   Greetings, my lady!

TAISA   You're late.

MAN   Don't be angry, my lady. The path is treacherous.

TAISA   I brought them both here.

MAN   Stupendous prey!

TAISA   Well, one of them didn't make it. He fell to his death.

MAN   The power of your eyes is dangerous, my lady.

TAISA   True.

MAN   May I dare ask whether it was the money in the sack that enticed them?

TAISA Yes.

MAN Such filth. Running after other people's money. Rotten thieves.

TAISA Go ahead, open it.

The man presses a lever, opening the hiding place that contains the treasures of all peoples who had visited this land. Taisa adorns herself in jewels and rich raiment.

Give me the little comb with the horse.

Taisa fastens the comb in her hair. The man falls to his knees.

MAN (*quietly*) When will I be free from this terrible power.... Damn you.

TAISA My supper.

The man crawls up to Volodya.

MAN Is he dead?!

TAISA The injection.

The man gives Volodya a shot. Volodya revives.

VOLODYA Oh, it's the whore.... All dressed up. Who wants to see your ugly face? (*Sees the open hiding place.*) What's this, New Year's Eve?

The man starts a fire in a hollow under Volodya, still pinned by the grate.

Oh, you monsters! Tatars! They're gonna fry me! Alive! Where's my sack? Give me my sack of money back, you old goat.

The man turns Volodya on a spit.

VOLODYA   Stop turning me, you bastard! I always knew you were a nasty little man. (*Choking on the smoke from the fire.*) It's shining. Just like in kindergarten. Like New Year's Eve. (*He sings.*) "When the white snow fell on thin ice." "The TU-140 is a very fast plane." They're going to celebrate New Year's Eve in kindergarten. I know Mama likes carnations and lilacs. Taisa Alanovna, Tolya cursed you. Tolya started it!!

TAISA   Let's see if he's done.

The man cuts a piece off Volodya.

MAN   Still a little tough.

Taisa sets the table.

VOLODYA   Oh, Mama, Vova's not gonna eat. Vova's stomach hurts....

TAISA   Where are my Genovese plates? You idiot! Where are my Genovese plates?

MAN   You smashed them at our last dinner, my lady.

TAISA   Liar! You're lying!

MAN   My lady, you got tired of them and threw them off the cliff, laughing the whole time.

TAISA   Serve the fruit and wine.

The man brings them to her and she eats.

Play something for me.

The man plays an exotic instrument. Taisa dances.

Red Paradise ⌇

VOLODYA "Rise in fiery flames, blue nights, we are pioneers, children of workers!"

TAISA Wine and spice!

> *The man gives Volodya wine and rubs spices in his wounds.*
> *Taisa dances again.*
> *Volodya is roasting.*

(*Angrily*) Well, is he going to be done soon or not? We should probably have marinated him in vinegar!

MAN Here's some Greek vinegar, my lady. It's first-class.

TAISA (*raises the bottle to Volodya's mouth*) Drink.

> *He tries to bite her.*

MAN Soak a sponge in vinegar, my lady. Otherwise he'll bite your fingers.

> *Taisa offers the sponge to Volodya on a spear.*
> *Volodya drinks, writhes in agony, and calms down.*

TAISA Is he dead? Turn him over.

> *The man turns Volodya on the spit. Taisa slices off a piece of flesh.*

That's better. Now add the spices.

> *She dances. Tolya crawls in.*

TOLYA I'm still alive! I'm still alive! I landed on the rocks. And the path leads right back up. There are crevasses everywhere. There's no way back. The sea is below. The everlasting sea surrounds us. Black sulfur oozes over the azure edge of the sea, dripping deadly sweat. There is no return. The sea is upside down. Fish are flying in the white sky. Swallows are stuck in the salty deep. The cliffs have changed place. The town below is suffused with red.

MAN   Goddammit! This one's crawled up, too.

Pokes him with a spear.

TOLYA   Help! Help! Don't! I'll wait on you. I'll serve you dinner. Please? Taisa Alanovna, spare me! It's drizzling outside, but it's warm and cozy in here. Let me stay?

TAISA   Let him stay.

MAN   You can serve us.

TOLYA (*crawls up*)   At your command, my lady.

TAISA   Turn your friend over, then. He's not cooking evenly.

TOLYA   This minute. Shall I stoke up the fire?

TAISA   Go ahead.

Tolik stokes the fire and roasts Volodya.

It smells good.

VOLODYA   Tolya, is that you?

TOLYA   He's alive, my lady!

TAISA   Break his head open with the axe. But make sure his brains don't spill out. I like them cooked with green peas.

VOLODYA   Don't, Tolik, please don't! I won't be able to see you anymore!

TOLYA   And why do you need to see me? (*He strikes him on the forehead with the axe.*)

VOLODYA   It's over. Darkness has set in. I've been tortured by Fascists. My heart has melted in a crucible of pain. Now it is soft and tender. I've died too often. Anguish and torment, they are mine. Fire has consumed me. The quest for happiness is spent. I am meat for the starving.

TOLYA (*anxiously*)   It's as if he's singing in Greek.

TAISA   Everybody sings the way he wants.

TOLYA   The sound of the sea is in his words.

VOLODYA   Flesh and bones have succumbed to torment. Alone the soul is preserved. The laughing soul, as pure as an innocent child. There are no tortures now. The immortal soul cannot be touched.

TOLYA   Aaaaa! (*He seizes a Genovese tray and hits Taisa on the head. She falls and dies.*)

MAN   Did you kill her?

TOLYA   Aaaaa! (*He kills the man the same way.*) I'll save you now, Vova.

VOLODYA   Don't. I don't care about living. It means nothing to me. I glimpsed a new life in the haze of my torments.

TOLYA   Oh, boy, it's hot. There's no way for me to get hold of you. You've been roasted all over. The bastards. They've stuffed you with dill.

VOLODYA   Ow, ow!

TOLYA   Hang on a minute, I'll get it all out, Vova. Just be still. It's a miracle you've come through. You have real courage.

VOLODYA   I'm almost dead from torture. What cannibals—

hankering after human flesh. And they enjoy it! Look at their faces—so pale and hard! But the soul can nourish only the one it belongs to.

TOLYA   You've survived it all!!! You're great! A hero, Vova. Drink! They have some kind of healing wine; it can do miracles.

VOLODYA   I want to see you. A blind man sees with his fingers. (*He feels Tolya's face.*) Yes, it's you, Anatoly. Give alms to the poor.

TOLYA   Alms? What alms, Vova? That bitch threw all the money off the cliff.

VOLODYA   There's treasure beyond belief stored in the cellars. We'll give it away—to nurseries, schools, hospitals.

TOLYA   No, there's something better. I've found you, Vova. I'll wash you and bandage you, and carry you down to the school. Let them see what a real man is made of! Otherwise they won't believe me. Everyone's out for himself! That's what they teach the children! It's appalling! But no more! You're what a human being should be! Let them follow your example!

VOLODYA   What's the point of glory or riches? Respect and friendship—true friendship—is what people need.

TOLYA   I'm your true friend, Vova!

Taisa comes to life.

TOLYA   She's alive!

He stabs her in the heart with a dagger. Taisa dies again with a peach in her mouth.

I've killed that snake, Vova! I've killed her!

The man comes to life.

And you, too! You rat! (*He kills him as he killed Taisa.*) Too bad about the rug though, the blood will soak it. Vova! You're so quiet! Speak, Vova. I'll get you out of here. You're the hope of the nation now. They'll put up a monument to you on Cosmonaut Street. They'll bow to your memory! Here, eat some grapes. You've lost a lot of blood.

VOLODYA   How can I eat? I'm the one who nourishes others. Thinking of others is what keeps me going.

TOLYA   Well, just you wait, bastards! They couldn't break you! They couldn't crush you! Keep on reflecting, Vova. Deep thoughts are your nature now. Why don't you lie down? You've suffered enough. Lie down for a while and gather your strength. I've put some grapes by your side. Keep thinking! No one will disturb you! I swear!

TAISA (*coming to life*)   It hurts. (*She looks at her blood.*) Now everything's going to get wet and slippery. We'll fall and break things.

TOLYA   What—you're not dead yet?!

TAISA   Don't shout. It hurts my ears. Everything's spinning.

TOLYA   Didn't I just stab you in the heart?

TAISA   No one dies here.

> *Tolya hits her on the head with the tray. She dies again.*

MAN (*coming to life*)   No one dies here.

> *Tolya hits him too and he dies again.*

TAISA (*coming to life*)   No one dies here.

Tolya hits Taisa and she dies again.

MAN (*reviving*)   No one dies here.

Tolya hits him and he dies, etc. The interludes between death
and life become shorter.
Tolya barely has time to hit each with the tray before
both come back to life.

TAISA AND MAN (*together*)   No one dies here!!!

Pause.

TAISA   But we really hurt and we're soaking wet.

MAN   You animal!

TOLYA   Who? Me? It's you who're the animal. Why do you torture people?

MAN   And you don't torture us?

TAISA   You attack us with knives.

TOLYA   Shut up, bitch.

TAISA   You insult and attack us. Now it hurts to move.

MAN   He cracked my head open.

TAISA   It hurts to breathe.

MAN   And I can't blink my eyes. I see flashes of light when I do.

TOLYA   So now *you're* complaining?

VOLODYA   Victory! Victory! Victory! Victory!

TOLYA   You haven't made him give in.

MAN   We wanted to eat him, then you barged in. Asshole.

TAISA   Let him go. It's stopped drizzling. He asked, and we let him in. Now he's no longer welcome. Go!

MAN   Go!

TOLYA   What are you—crazy? Look what you did to that man over there!

TAISA   No one invited you. And you attack people with knives.

MAN   And crack their heads open. It hurts to blink.

TAISA   But we didn't touch you. We let you in from the rain.

MAN   And now we're sorry.

TOLYA   Ohhhh! (*He seizes the dagger and stabs himself.*)

TAISA   No one dies here!

MAN   It'll be even wetter with blood.

They wait. Tolya does not come back to life.

VOLODYA   Victory! Victory! Soon there will be Victory! Everything will be given away. It's victory for the people!

TAISA   He's not reviving.

MAN   Probably just pretending.

TAISA   Poke him.

MAN (*poking Tolya*)   Me first!

TAISA   No, me!

MAN   I said, me first! Or I'll smash your face in.

TAISA   Me first! Me first! Me first!

MAN   All right, go ahead. You first.

TAISA   I'm the lady of the house.

MAN   Go ahead, quick! What're you gonna use?

TAISA   Give me that scalpel over there. The narrow one. (*She stabs herself.*)

MAN   Well, this takes courage, but I can do it. If I can only reach. It hurts to crawl. Aha, here are some little scissors. Just right. (*He cuts his stomach open.*)

VOLODYA   Everybody! Everybody! Everybody! It's a universal victory for the people! The victory is for the people. Give everything, everything that's good to the people. Give them everything. They have nothing. To everyone! To everyone! To everyone! Victory for the people! Victory!

Everybody comes back to life.

TOLYA   Ohhh. I'm alive again.

He cries.

TAISA   No one dies here!

TOLYA   You don't have to tell *me* that. And don't splatter me with your blood!

TAISA   And who stabbed me? Here, is this what you want?

She drizzles her blood on him.

TOLYA (*with hatred*)   Let me die, bitch!

MAN   Go ahead and try! Just try! You managed to be out longer than anyone else. Try it again. Try a different way.

TOLYA   What's all this hanging out of your stomach? It's disgusting.

MAN   Give me that little towel over there. That white one. Throw it over here.

TOLYA   It hurts to move.

MAN   Everybody hurts. Just reach for that towel and throw it to me.

TOLYA   Ugh, gross. You spilled your guts all over the floor. Patch
yourself up.

MAN (*bandaging himself up*)   Thank you. I got weak. A terrible way
to feel. Look at all that blood! Who's gonna clean it up? The rug
has to be thrown out altogether.

TAISA   I will not give that rug away!

MAN   It can't be saved. It's soaked. It'll be full of worms.

TAISA   Ugh.

MAN (*to Tolya*)   Hey, roll up the rug.

TOLYA   Do I look like your servant? "Throw me the towel. Roll up
the rug."

MAN   Better roll it up, or the worms will crawl into your wounds
and make you itch.

TOLYA (*with hatred*)   I've never seen such bastards!

MAN   Scratch out your eyes. You'll feel a little better. Need any
help with that?

TOLYA   Go away! Keep your hands off me!

MAN   Then go to work. Take your time. Take breaks. No one's
hurrying you. It's heavy. It's wet. Start from the other end.

They roll up the rug.

MAN   There's some writing down there on the floor. Half-formed
letters. Read it, all right? If you can read, that is. Watch out,
you'll drip blood all over it! The letters will get smeared.

TOLYA   What can it be? You've made it up.

MAN   Read it, read it!

TOLYA (*reads*)   The ... there ... will....

MAN   Move over. Maybe there's another treasure?

Tolya temporarily kills the Man.

TOLYA   He's obsessed by this "treasure." Taiska, help me wipe the blood off the letters.

TAISA   I keep wiping it off, but the blood keeps coming. Just look at the hole you've made in me!

TOLYA   You're such a baby. Can't do anything for yourself. Stuff cotton wool inside the wound. There! Push it deeper!

TAISA   It's getting soaked. I'd better clamp it.

She closes the wound with surgical clamps.

TOLYA   Don't be stupid, Taiska. The clamps catch on things.

TAISA   I'm comfortable this way.

TOLYA   All right, but keep on wiping.

Taisa wipes the floor.

TOLYA (*reads*)   "There will come ... come a day...." Aha, aha, there will come a day, "blo ... d" blood, probably, yes! (*He reads.*) "Bloo ... d," well, I see now: "There will come a day when the blood of the centuries will rise from the depths and you will no longer die." What else? That's it. What? That's it?! How can it be? Taiska, what does it mean? Who wrote this? What are you staring at?

Taisa looks upwards.

TOLYA What—are you paralyzed or something?

TAISA Let's hang ourselves.

TOLYA I can't stand it anymore.

VOLODYA "No" to war, "yes" to peace! "No" to war, "yes" to peace! Peace to the world! Peace to the world! Give everything to the people. Everything, everything, everything. And there will be peace on earth. Laughter for children and bread for pigeons. Shelter for the old. Training for the young. Fight for peace, for the happiness of the people. Fight! Fight! Fight! Fight!

TAISA Maybe we should … do something….

TOLYA Don't you dare touch him!

TAISA There's a buzzing noise coming off him.

TOLYA Hands off! He's the only one who…. Do you understand?

TAISA Well, all right. I was just thinking that we haven't hanged ourselves yet. We've only been stabbed with knives and roasted on a spit. Maybe this will work? If we cut off the air supply, the blood won't be able to get to our muscles. It will coagulate. Our brains will shut down. Then we'll really be dead. (*She adjusts the noose.*) Tolik, Tolik, if only you hadn't stabbed me, I could have made a better noose. But it's all twisted.

TOLYA That doesn't matter. Just make it strong.

TAISA It's strong. These hooks will hold. (*She sticks her head through the noose.*) They're solid.

TOLYA Wait! Why do you get to go first? You have to wait your turn! The man hasn't revived yet. And we have to hang Vova, since he can't do it for himself. His hands are burnt and his eyes are gone.

VOLODYA   I can see!

TOLYA (*shaking*)   My God! What a hero! A real hero!

VOLODYA   I can see! I can see! I can see!

He runs into the wall and dies.

MAN (*coming back to life*)   What's all this yelling and rushing about? And who stepped on my guts, tell me that!

TOLYA   It was Vova. He's blind. But that's all right, you'll manage. You're nothing, and he's a real man!

He leans over Volodya.

MAN   What's new?

TOLYA   Shut up. Can't you see he's dead?

MAN   No. Really?

TOLYA   You pig, mocking the death of a man like this. Get up! And take your hat off!

MAN   I don't have a hat.

TAISA   All right, then, I'm going first. I'm not waiting around. Who knows when this one will revive.

MAN   Are you gonna jump? You can't kill yourself falling off the cliff.

TOLYA (*to the Man*)   It's all set. We're going to hang ourselves. There's no other way out. And we're not going to wait for Vova to wake up. We're going to have to hang him ourselves. Help us.

They hang the dead Vova. Then they hang themselves. Agony.
The distant splash of water can be heard. It's is getting closer.
It's on the floor. It's rising higher, up to the feet of the hanged.

It's blood.

TOLYA (*opening his eyes*)   I'm alive again. I knew it. What's that? Am I seeing red or is something ... there? Hey, has anyone come back to life? (*He swings on the rope and pushes everybody.*) We're drowning! We're drowning! Help! It's a flood!

Everybody starts rocking, knocking into each other,
and coming back to life.

VOLODYA   I see! I see! I see the light!

TAISA   The rope is suffocating me. It's because the noose is twisted. It's all your fault, Tolik.

TOLYA   We're drowning! Drowning! We have to get down!

MAN   How? We're too slippery, there's nothing to grab on to.

TOLYA   Maybe we'll drown, huh? This is blood, after all, not water. I almost drowned once in the Black Sea. My lungs got scorched. But this is blood!

MAN   Ow, my guts are hanging out. I feel nauseous, like in an airplane.

TOLYA   I'm sick and tired of your complaints.

He knocks against the man.

MAN   Don't spin me around, I beg you! Don't!

TOLYA   Maybe we'll drown in this blood, huh?

TAISA   I feel nauseous, too. I can't stand the sight of blood. It makes me dizzy.

TOLYA   Now you're complaining, too?

He hits Taisa.

TAISA   I'll stop, I promise! I feel fine.

VOLODYA   I can see! I can see!

MAN   Shut up, you, undercooked grub!

TAISA   We should have roasted you longer!

TOLYA   How dare you! Pigs!

They all fight and get entangled with each other.

VOLODYA   I can see! I see a purple palace!

TOLYA (*to Taisa*)   Let go of me. Sort yourself out.

MAN   Stop pulling at me! You're tearing my guts out!

VOLODYA   I am slowly ascending to the purple palace!

TOLYA   Taiska, come on, cooperate!

TAISA   No. I like twisting around with you.

VOLODYA   I've arrived, I've arrived at the purple palace!

TOLYA   Taiska, let go of me! Go over to him. (*He pushes her away toward the Man.*)

TAISA   I'm tired of hanging! Someone let me down!

MAN   My lady, stop it. You're making waves of blood.

TOLYA   It's scorching me.

MAN   Everything scorches you. The Black Sea. The blood.

TOLYA   This is blood of the ages. It is scalding me! Hooray!

MAN   Are you out of your mind? What are you so happy about? Extra pain? My intestines have fallen out. I'm empty. Like a gutted fish.

TOLYA   Taisa, kick around some more. Push a wave over to me.

Taisa twists and turns on the rope. Waves of blood wash Tolya apart. He laughs.

MAN   Oh, yes, how funny.

TOLYA   It tickles!

MAN   Sure, keep on laughing.

VOLODYA   Palace, oh palace, open your doors! Are you there for the people? This is a palace for the people! Hurry, hurry! People, people, hurry!

TOLYA   It's eating us! Guys, we're saved! It's eating us!

MAN   Stop telling lies! We'll never stop suffering. We don't need false hope.

TOLYA   Look. Are your guts touching the blood?

MAN   Can't you see for yourself?

TOLYA   The parts of you covered by blood—look!

MAN   What?

TOLYA   The parts the blood has reached—what happens to them?

MAN (*brings his guts closer*)   It's like they're cut off! No! Half my guts have been eaten away.

TOLYA   And now take a look at your feet!

MAN   Right down to the bone! How can this be? We're dissolving???

TOLYA   Yes. It's like acid. It's so old, it goes back to our forefathers. Look how the blood is churning.

VOLODYA   I can see! I can see! People are pouring into the purple palace. Pouring! Pouring! I'm floating in purple!

TAISA   You're lying. I've floated in purple before and nothing happened. We can't die.

MAN   It's all right, my lady. This blood is dissolving us.

TOLYA   What's this? Is it subsiding? Oh no, it's receding!

Everyone screams and cries.

Everybody be quiet! Shut up! Pretend you don't care.

MAN   I spit on this blood.

TAISA   Stupid red puddle.

VOLODYA   I'm flying away!

TOLYA   Don't. You have to fear death. That's the secret.

MAN   He's rejoicing. We'd better knock him out for awhile.

TOLYA   Don't you dare touch him! He's the only one who wants his death to mean something! All you can think about is yourself.

MAN   He's scaring off the blood. It's subsiding!

TOLYA   Keep trying! Fear death. You have to be afraid of dying. Let *it* want *us*. (*Screaming.*) Stop! Stop! God, no!

MAN   If only we can live just a little bit longer! Just a minute! One little instant! An instant!

TAISA   I'm not going to die! I want to live. I want a watermelon!

They struggle and knock against each other, afraid to die.

VOLODYA   Purple! Waves of purple. People in purple. I'm flying, flying, fly....

The blood is rising. It has reached the ceiling of the tower. Sobbing and gurgling are heard. Thrashing. Silence. Everything is still. Blood saturates everything in deep red. It subsides. It is gone. Empty nooses hang in the empty room washed in blood. The sun dries out the room. A bird flies in. It starts singing.

CURTAIN

Translated from the Russian
*by **Nadya L. Peterson** and **Kathryn Szczepanska***

THE WITCHING HOUR

A Play in Two Acts

CHARACTERS

LIDYA PETROVNA

THE WOMAN

ALEKSANDER IVANOVICH

OLYA CHERKASOVA

ELENA MAXIMOVNA

GENA ESKIN

The Witching Hour

ACT I: *THE FIELD*

State farm potato field. A yellow autumn grove in the distance. Gray skies. Chilly. Monotonous, barren landscape. Lidya Petrovna is making her way through the field. She's been sent with her colleagues to harvest potatoes. She's lost her way.

LIDYA PETROVNA Now what?... I might break my legs and no one would know.There's nowhere to go ... what did they say — go straight, and keep going straight. It's straight all right, but I don't see a thing. Where is everyone? (*Yells out.*) Comrades! Aleksander Ivanovich! (*After a brief pause.*) I must be crazy to yell in an empty field. Maybe they're in a different field? Ours is a potato field. (*Picks up a potato.*) But I'm in a potato field. Oy-ey-ey-ey, who would treat potatoes this way? They'll all rot, poor things.

> *Lidya Petrovna suddenly notices a woman, who has been jumping over the bumps and ditches alongside her for some time.*

Hey! Lady ... eh ... M'am, M'am! Wait up! Wait! You're from around here, aren't you? Oh, my.... Thank goodness! Where did you come from.... I'm lost. Can you tell me how to get to the third sector? Is this the third sector?... I can't tell anything.... No one is around, I don't know why....

THE WOMAN You're here.

LIDYA PETROVNA (*slightly startled*) Me? Well, yes, I'm here. I need to know.... How do I get to the third sector? We've been sent

for the harvest.... I was late, and everybody had already left....
And no one tells me anything, I'm so confused now. Why don't
you speak? I don't even know your name.

THE WOMAN   Call me Auntie.

LIDYA PETROVNA (*after a pause*)   All right. I need the third sector.
Where is it?

THE WOMAN   Over there! (*Waves her hand in a vague direction.*)

LIDYA PETROVNA   Over where? I don't understand.

The Woman giggles.

You state farmers are strange people.... Do you want help with
the harvest or not? Why are you laughing? We didn't ask to
come here....

Continues to walk. The Woman walks alongside, giggling.

So, is this the right way?

THE WOMAN (*cheerfully*)   That way! That way!

LIDYA PETROVNA   This is awful. They weren't prepared for us
at all. The cafeteria's dreadful; I didn't even want to get in. It's
depressing, and cold, and dirty here. And our girls ... oh ... your
legs are bare. You could catch cold. You shouldn't walk around
in galoshes without stockings....Well, I don't know.... it's awful,
simply awful....

THE WOMAN (*sobbing*)   You're so nice!

LIDYA PETROVNA   Oh dear, what's the matter with you? Don't
you have any stockings?

THE WOMAN   No.

The Witching Hour ⌐

LIDYA PETROVNA   How come? It's October. I don't understand. I'm telling you this as a woman. If you get numb from cold down there, it will make you sterile. It's no joke walking around with bare legs in October.

> *The Woman gives her a timid, questioning look out*
> *of the corner of her eye.*

If you want, I could ... I could give you some stockings . ..but it's just so strange.

THE WOMAN   I want.

LIDYA PETROVNA   Well, not now, of course! I don't carry around an extra pair of stockings.

THE WOMAN   Now!

LIDYA PETROVNA   Excuse me?

> *The Woman laughs; Lidya Petrovna looks closely at her with pity.*

Ah, I see ... you poor thing ... you're one of those.... I didn't notice right away, your face looks normal ... but it's hard to tell sometimes. And you don't have anyone looking after you, taking care of you? There must be somebody!

THE WOMAN   You are.

LIDYA PETROVNA (*touched*)   There, there, my dear.... I'll be leaving for the city soon, I have a family there, a job. Let me tie your scarf. (*Fixes it.*) The wind doesn't bother you? Are you cold?

THE WOMAN   You won't leave....

LIDYA PETROVNA   And I'll give you the stockings. Come to the cafeteria at lunchtime, and I'll bring them. Will you come?

The Woman nods vigorously, licking her lips.

Maybe you're hungry. Do you want to eat?

THE WOMAN   I want.

LIDYA PETROVNA   They don't feed you, do they? You must live in some kind of institution. Is there a place for people like you around here? Where do you live?

THE WOMAN (*laughs lightly and merrily*)   Everywhere!

LIDYA PETROVNA (*laughs involuntarily*)   A simple child of God.... You don't ask for anything, don't feel the cold, don't need to eat....

THE WOMAN   I need you.

LIDYA PETROVNA   I'll get you the stockings. I have a good pair, woolen. I've only worn them once. What's your name? Do you know it?

THE WOMAN   I know.

LIDYA PETROVNA   So, what is it?

THE WOMAN   Slayer.

LIDYA PETROVNA (*after a pause*)   That's a strange name. Is it Ukrainian or something? Oh, where is that third sector? I'll keep trying anyway.

They continue to walk. The Woman peers into her face with curiosity.

Why are you looking at me like that, dear?

The Witching Hour ⌒

THE WOMAN (*angrily*)   I told you! Call me Auntie!

LIDYA PETROVNA   But how can I call you that? We're about the same age....

THE WOMAN (*screaming*)   Auntie, I said!

LIDYA PETROVNA (*cautiously*)   All right, all right, just calm down.... Auntie.... Ay, what's this?

She stops, holding her chest.

THE WOMAN (*sympathetically*)   Does it ache?

LIDYA PETROVNA   What? Yes, sort of ... such a horrible feeling.

THE WOMAN (*jumping around the bumps and ditches*)   Aching! Our Lida's heart is aching!

LIDYA PETROVNA (*wearily*)   She's completely mad. She could knock me right over! (*Startled.*) How did you know my name?

The woman does not answer her, singing a strange wild song.

She must have heard that in the cafeteria. How else could she, a simple child of God.... Wanders around, just looking at people.... So, where is this road, anyway? I should have found it by now....

THE WOMAN (*singing*)   Oh, road, my dear road, my little road....

LIDYA PETROVNA (*yelling*)   Shut up now, will ya! I'm going to go crazy!

THE WOMAN (*firm and with authority*)   No, you're not!

LIDYA PETROVNA   You're so strange ... too strange somehow.... Auntie, ah! (*Holds her chest.*)

THE WOMAN   Aching, is it?

LIDYA PETROVNA   Who are you?

THE WOMAN   Slayer.

LIDYA PETROVNA   What do you mean, Slayer? Where did you come from? I was walking along by myself. Why didn't I see you? You appeared out of nowhere. (*Steps back.*) Where did you come from?

THE WOMAN   From everywhere!

LIDYA PETROVNA (*suddenly*)   Oh, this is awful!

THE WOMAN (*rejoicing*)   Aching! It's breaking!

LIDYA PETROVNA   What's happening? Where's the road? Where's the third sector? If only Aleksander Ivanovich were here. Where has the road gone?

THE WOMAN   The road has disappeared.

LIDYA PETROVNA   The road disappeared? Where? What do you mean?

THE WOMAN   It slid away.... Got tired, you know, all trampled down....

LIDYA PETROVNA   The road ... tired.... (*sits down on a mound*) My kidneys will freeze. How is this possible? If you go somewhere, you should get there eventually. But this field seems unending....

THE WOMAN   I'm leading you in circles.

LIDYA PETROVNA   Why do that?

THE WOMAN   Just because. It's nice here! The open air! Oohh!

LIDYA PETROVNA   Yeah, right ... it's nice here ... maybe for a lunatic like you.

The Witching Hour

THE WOMAN   I'll lead you around a bit more, all right?

LIDYA PETROVNA   Just leave me alone.

THE WOMAN   Only for a little while. It's nice here. It's bright.

LIDYA PETROVNA   Why don't they send younger people to help out on the farm? They shouldn't do this to us, they don't have the right! They simply torture people!

THE WOMAN   Just a little. I'll just fool around with you a little, all right?

LIDYA PETROVNA   What an intolerable, stupid, crazy woman!

THE WOMAN (*fierce*)   Auntie, I said!

LIDYA PETROVNA   What's it to you?

THE WOMAN   It sounds nice.

LIDYA PETROVNA   Do you think you're a witch, a sorceress?

THE WOMAN   NO-no-no! Not at all! I don't know anything about such things.

LIDYA PETROVNA   Then why are you trying to scare me?

THE WOMAN (*whining*)   Only a little.

LIDYA PETROVNA   Why are you pestering me? What do you want?

THE WOMAN (*evasively*)   You're fun.

LIDYA PETROVNA   I'm fun when I'm together with my comrades on a straight road, but here, in the middle of a field, with you, a mad woman, I'm not fun. She wants to lead me around! Nonsense!

THE WOMAN   All right then. Go your own way, if you want. (*jumps on a high mound*) Just go straight ahead, keep going straight ahead all the time, follow the wind. See it?

LIDYA PETROVNA   I don't see anything.

THE WOMAN   You blind fool!

LIDYA PETROVNA   This is a nightmare … now she's calling me names….

THE WOMAN   There's the wind. It's coming now….

The wind begins to blow.

See, you can go in that direction. The wind is showing you the way.

LIDYA PETROVNA   All right, I'll go then. I'll go where the wind is showing me the way.

She walks.

THE WOMAN (*to her back*)   I'm the Evil of the World!

LIDYA PETROVNA   Oh.

THE WOMAN   Just look at her, running away! I'm the Slayer-woman, I keep the world in fear! America is afraid of me, the whole world is afraid of me, everyone is, but not you, stupid woman.

Lidya Petrovna returns.

LIDYA PETROVNA   There's nothing there.

THE WOMAN   Scared, are you?

LIDYA PETROVNA   There was a grove, way off. But I can't see it anymore.

THE WOMAN   Didn't I tell you?

LIDYA PETROVNA   Who are you?

The Witching Hour ⌢

THE WOMAN   I'm telling a secret! Achtung, Achtung! Listen up! I'm the Evil of the World! Hurrah!

LIDYA PETROVNA   You, the Evil of the World? You must be kidding. Look at yourself—you pitiful creature.

THE WOMAN   Shut up, stupid! What d'ya know? What d'ya know?

> *The Woman is galloping around the field,*
> *throwing potatoes at Lidya Petrovna.*

LIDYA PETROVNA   Hey, hey, you just stop it!

THE WOMAN (*comes up to her*)   I'm out of breath. Here's what we do. I'm running away. You have to catch me. If you do—there will be heaven on earth, and if you don't—it's the end of the world. Got it?

LIDYA PETROVNA   Got it.

THE WOMAN   So—come and get me! (*Runs away.*) Well? Come on! Catch me!

LIDYA PETROVNA (*to herself*)   All right…. Basically, we've been sent to harvest potatoes. The whole office. Our collective. I was late. And then I got lost. I started walking. I ran into a woman with bare legs. She's—the Evil of the World. And if I catch her—there will be heaven on earth…. (*Looks around.*) And yet, I wonder. People are so mysterious. I don't believe that she's the Evil of the World, but … but I'll catch her just in case….

THE WOMAN   Don't worry about people! Just catch me! Come on, Lida, come on!

The woman runs around. Lidya Petrovna runs after her.
The Woman squeals, laughs out loud, sings wildly.

Lida, Lida, keep on trying, if you stop there's only dying. You only get one try, Lidushka!

All of a sudden, the Woman trips and falls down on her back.
Lidya Petrovna has almost caught up to her.
The Woman, with her legs in the air, waves her away.

Don't touch me! If you touch me, you will rot!

LIDYA PETROVNA (*jumps aside*)   Ai!

THE WOMAN (*gets to her feet at once, stern*)   That's it, Lida.

They stand, facing each other.

(*Sings.*) Lost her nerve, it doesn't pay, hope and heaven's gone away! Eh-he-he-eh, fooled you, Lida!

LIDYA PETROVNA   What do you want from me?

THE WOMAN   Lida, only you would rot, like potatoes in dirt, but everything else would bloom forever. Forever, Lida, like angels in heaven, like apple trees in spring, like God's flowers.

LIDYA PETROVNA (*carefully approaching her*)   So I'll catch you!

The Woman stands still.

THE WOMAN   Do you know how annoying this is? How many times have I told you to catch me! How many chances have I given you? On purpose! You think I wasn't afraid? I'd have died! But I was brave and I gave you the chances. And now everything is fine—I get to live.

Lidya Petrovna grabs the Woman.

The Witching Hour ⌒

LIDYA PETROVNA   I got you.

THE WOMAN   Stop screaming?! You'll make me deaf!

LIDYA PETROVNA   I've got you, you wretched woman! (*Shakes her.*)

THE WOMAN   Oh, oh, let go of me! You're hurting me! You're making my head spin!

LIDYA PETROVNA (*lets go of the Woman*)   Really, what am I doing….I'm losing my mind…. I'm chasing a sick woman, and I'm freezing, and I can't find my colleagues….

THE WOMAN   Let's howl together! (*Howls.*) It's a mournful howl.

LIDYA PETROVNA   What? Forgive me, dear. When you come around, I'll get you the stockings. I'm going now, I have to go, good bye.

THE WOMAN   So be it. Fall into the pit!

A pit opens up and Lidya Petrovna falls into the pit and suddenly disappears. The Woman goes up to the edge and looks in.

You didn't hurt yourself, did you?

LIDYA PETROVNA (*from below*)   Help, get me out of here right now! I hurt myself. Hurry!

THE WOMAN (*sits down on the edge of the pit*)   Why don't you rest a bit, lie down. There's some hay, very good hay down there, I gathered it just for you. There, in the corner. Lie down for a while. (*Laughs, dangling her legs in the air.*) Don't touch my feet, don't! I'm ticklish! (*Drops one boot into the pit.*) Give me my boot! Lida, give me back my boot!

LIDYA PETROVNA   Not until you get me out of here.

165

THE WOMAN   But I'm barefoot!

LIDYA PETROVNA   I don't care!

THE WOMAN   But I'll catch cold. The ground is freezing! It's almost winter!

LIDYA PETROVNA   Get me out of here!

THE WOMAN   Just hold on! So many things are about to happen here! Hold on, Lida! You've changed everything, anyway....

LIDYA PETROVNA   I'm not waiting.

THE WOMAN   Where do you think you're going? Where? Stop pushing on the wall, you'll move it, Lida! You'll move the world! Lida-a-a-a!

> *The walls of the pit begin to open, and the Woman rushes away on the crest of the wave of earth. The pit walls spread apart and slide off, like a potato peel, revealing a bare, smooth and rosy young earth with Lidya Petrovna standing on it.*

LIDYA PETROVNA (*looking at the Woman, disappearing in the distance*)   Aha! Away you go! Falling! Whirling! Smash, crash into the horizon! Paint the sky with blood!

> *The Woman is standing behind her.*

THE WOMAN   Give me back my boot! (*Grabs it and puts it on.*)

LIDYA PETROVNA   I know what you are. You're some kind of natural force.

THE WOMAN   Then why am I an Auntie?

LIDYA PETROVNA   That I don't know. But you're not human. You're ... why is the ground like this? What happened?

The Witching Hour

THE WOMAN   The surface layer slid away.

LIDYA PETROVNA   Where to?

THE WOMAN   Into the ocean.

LIDYA PETROVNA   What ocean?

THE WOMAN   Ignorant woman! Where does the earth drift?

LIDYA PETROVNA   The Earth drifts in space.

THE WOMAN   Sure, sure, in space. I hurt my foot all because of you.

LIDYA PETROVNA   The earth drifts in space! Stupid hag!

THE WOMAN   It drifts in the ocean, Lida. Resting upon three whales. Its skin peeled and slid off. It's all new now, fresh as an apple, smooth like baby skin. (*Pats the earth.*) There, my baby, there my dear, don't tremble like this, darling, don't be afraid, no one's gonna hurt you now....

LIDYA PETROVNA   But why three whales?... They said—space, the universe....

THE WOMAN   The universe ... they said ... so you wouldn't get bored. They gave you toys to play with. Use your brain. You must think. All right, I'm done with this. That's it! No more!

LIDYA PETROVNA (*looks around*)   Where is the farm?

THE WOMAN   It slid away.

LIDYA PETROVNA   And where ... where is everybody?

THE WOMAN   Gone, gone!

LIDYA PETROVNA   But who is left?

THE WOMAN   You are.

LIDYA PETROVNA   And I'm all alone?

THE WOMAN   You're all alone.

LIDYA PETROVNA   But why? What have I done to be left all alone? Take me. Make me go away … like everybody else! Throw me where you threw the rest! Take me there, you wicked woman! Vile creature! Take me away!

THE WOMAN   I am not the one who takes away. I don't have the power.

LIDYA PETROVNA   Then who has?

THE WOMAN   Who, who? How should I know that?

LIDYA PETROVNA   Who's doing all this? (*Looks around.*)

THE WOMAN   I don't know. (*Looks around too.*) Shall we howl?!

LIDYA PETROVNA   Not now. So, you don't know either?

THE WOMAN   You think I wouldn't have told you? I'd have told you right away: this and that, such and such is the person who is doing this…. But I have no idea.

LIDYA PETROVNA   Listen to me. We have to do something. Let's find this person. I don't know, we have to do something. Maybe this is all just a dream?

THE WOMAN   Of course, it's a dream.

LIDYA PETROVNA   Anyway, come on, let's go.

Drags the Woman along.

THE WOMAN   Where are we going?

LIDYA PETROVNA   To look for this person.

THE WOMAN   Who?

LIDYA PETROVNA   The one who is doing this!

THE WOMAN Doing what?

LIDYA PETROVNA Well … peeling off the earth's surface … and all … let's go.

THE WOMAN But how? Just look, the earth is tender where we walk on her, she's not used to it yet.

LIDYA PETROVNA Who?

THE WOMAN Who, who? Who are you standing on?

LIDYA PETROVNA I'm standing on the earth.

THE WOMAN And if someone stood on you, what would you say?

LIDYA PETROVNA We'll walk carefully, on our tippy toes.

THE WOMAN And where can we go? We'll get to the edge, where the ocean is…. And we'll swim away…. What then? Where could we, two women, get to….

LIDYA PETROVNA First of all, you aren't a woman … you're … I don't know what you are. And also, we must tell the others, the people.

THE WOMAN There are no others, Lida. You're the only one left.

LIDYA PETROVNA Why am I left alone? For whom?

THE WOMAN For me.

LIDYA PETROVNA I was left for you?

THE WOMAN Well. I pushed you into that pit, so you wouldn't get carried off.

LIDYA PETROVNA Why do you need me?

THE WOMAN I can't be without you. All the others died. If you die, I die. I'm—the Evil of the World. I gobble people up and rejoice in it, but when everyone is gone, I'll die. Now, that's how it is. You're the last one left. I'll take good care of you. I'll eat you little by little. And we'll live! It's all fine! It's nice here, it's bright in the open air!

Lidya Petrovna turns away from her.

Come on, Lida! Lida! Don't leave me alone! Look, I'm a birch-tree! (*Assumes a fanciful pose.*)

LIDYA PETROVNA   I'm not going to live.

THE WOMAN   You are. You have kids. And a husband.

LIDYA PETROVNA   So, they ... they still exist?

THE WOMAN   They do, they do.

LIDYA PETROVNA   Then you lied about everything? They still exist?

THE WOMAN   Yes! They do! Everybody does! Everything's for you, my queen! Just as if they were real! Oh, my queen! Just as if they were alive! Just don't die, Lida, all right? No dying? And don't get bored, all right?

LIDYA PETROVNA   Wait, hold on, so they exist?

THE WOMAN   It is just like they're real! To the last detail. No one could tell the difference! You won't die, will you? And you won't be bored?

LIDYA PETROVNA   Like real? My children, just like real? Vovochka, Svetlanka, my husband? Aleksander Ivanovich, and Olya Cherkasova?

THE WOMAN   Just like real!

LIDYA PETROVNA   And where do I live?

THE WOMAN   Anywhere you want! Want a mansion downtown?

LIDYA PETROVNA   I want it the way it was.

THE WOMAN   It is as it was. You want the right thing. Good girl. Don't die, all right? Don't be bored?

LIDYA PETROVNA   No. I'll live. I don't believe you. No. (*Leaves.*)

THE WOMAN (*to her back*)   Lida, Lida, don't look in their eyes for too long. Don't look into them, Lidushka, my sweetheart, my precious!

ACT II: *THE OFFICE*

An Engineers' Office. Desks, drawing boards, windows, doorways, telephones, file cabinets, workers. Beginning of a work day. Everyone is sitting at his desk. Lidya Petrovna enters.

LIDYA PETROVNA   Hello.

Disorderly chorus of greetings

OLYA   Ah, I can't go on like this anymore!

ELENA MAXIMOVNA (*calling her to order*)   Olya!

OLYA   No, let Lidya Petrovna explain. Lidya Petrovna, what do we live for?

GENA   I know what Olya lives for!

OLYA   No one's asking you, Gena! So, Lidya Petrovna, please tell us!

LIDYA PETROVNA (*suspiciously*)   Olya, you've never asked such a question before.

OLYA   Before what?

LIDYA PETROVNA   Before the potatoes.

OLYA   Before the potatoes. You and your potatoes!

ALEKSANDER IVANOVICH   Olya, get to work, please. We have only two days to finish the project, and your blueprint isn't ready yet.

OLYA   The hell with it.

ELENA MAXIMOVNA   You're out of line, Olya. Everyone is working. You're the only one who isn't. Perhaps the others don't want to work either.

OLYA   I want to work. But not before I know what we all live for. Why live? Tell me, why?

ELENA MAXIMOVNA   What do you mean, why? No one's asking you. You live because you were born.

OLYA   Well, I'm young, I'm curious, it stands to reason. It's something only young people are interested in, I know. But still, while I'm young, I'm interested. I'm scared of getting old.

ELENA MAXIMOVNA   There you go, you just answered your own question. You live to be young.

OLYA   That's not an answer! What do *you* live for, then?

ELENA MAXIMOVNA   That's my business. I don't have to answer that.

ALEKSANDER IVANOVICH   Comrades, comrades, let's leave the chatter for the lunch break. I'm getting a headache!

GENA   In my opinion, young women should not be kept in cages.

OLYA   What do you mean, cages?

GENA   They should not have to work in offices. It's the duty of the government to provide security for young women. They should be able to wander at will in the fields among the flowers.

LIDYA PETROVNA (*hastily*)   No, No!

Pause.

GENA   Why don't you answer the question, Lidya Petrovna?

LIDYA PETROVNA   What? No, all I'm saying is that this is a very odd conversation we're having.

ELENA MAXIMOVNA   Olya must think because she's young, she can act like a spoiled child.

OLYA   What do you mean, Elena Maximovna?! When I went to bed yesterday evening, I was so sad. So sad....

LIDYA PETROVNA   Why?

OLYA   All of a sudden, I thought: Why do I live? I cried all night.

GENA   It's growing pains.

LIDYA PETROVNA   Ah, what's that on your face? Wait, Olya, your mascara got smudged, let me take a look.

Comes up to Olya, takes her face in the hands, turns to the light, looks her in the eyes. Takes a step back.

She's alive, alive....alive to the very core. I don't see anything different.

OLYA   What's wrong with you? Your hands are shaking. What's wrong, Lidya Petrovna? Aren't you feeling well? You're pale.

LIDYA PETROVNA   No. My Svetochka is sick. Sore throat, that's all. I'm worried.

OLYA   Aleksander Ivanovich!

ALEKSANDER IVANOVICH: Yes, Olya.

OLYA   Let Lidya Petrovna go home! Her child is sick.

LIDYA PETROVNA   No, no! I don't want to!

ALEKSANDER IVANOVICH (*softly*)   Go home, Lidya Petrovna You won't be able to work anyway.

LIDYA PETROVNA   Of course I will.

ELENA MAXIMOVNA   No, you won't. Yesterday your calculations were all wrong again. You haven't been able to work for some time now. Not since the trip to the potato farm.

Pause

OLYA   You shouldn't say that!

LIDYA PETROVNA   It's not important. Svetochka will get better. She gargles, she is under doctor's orders. I'm just worried that Vovochka might get sick too. That's all.

ELENA MAXIMOVNA   Has her throat been sore for the last month?

LIDYA PETROVNA   No. Why?

ELENA MAXIMOVNA   Because the entire month now you haven't been yourself. Not since....

OLYA   I don't want to hear about potatoes anymore! (*Runs out, slamming the door.*)

ALEKSANDER IVANOVICH   Really, comrades, why all this tension? Let's mind our own business. Lidya Petrovna, you can go home if you like.

LIDYA PETROVNA (*sadly*)   It won't help.

Pause

GENA   Lidya Petrovna, do you need anything? Can I get something for you?

LIDYA PETROVNA   Like what?

GENA   Maybe groceries. So you wouldn't have to go shopping after work.

LIDYA PETROVNA   This can't be happening.

GENA   What can't be happening?

LIDYA PETROVNA (*shakes her head, stands up and comes up to Gena Eskin*)   This can't be happening. (*Looks into his eyes.*) Alive, alive, alive—to the very core. And I don't see anything different.

Uneasy silence.

GENA   I'm going out for a smoke.

ELENA MAXIMOVNA (*meaningfully*)   I'm coming with you. (*Loud enough to be heard.*) Let's leave them alone. (*They leave.*)

ALEKSANDER IVANOVICH   Lidya Petrovna, what's the matter?

LIDYA PETROVNA   I don't want to talk about it.

ALEKSANDER IVANOVICH (*softly*)   Lidya Petrovna, please?

LIDYA PETROVNA (*affirmatively*)   He seems so real.

ALEKSANDER IVANOVICH   What do you mean, Lidya Petrovna? How so?

LIDYA PETROVNA   Aleksander Ivanovich, I trust you more than … more than anybody in the world.

ALEKSANDER IVANOVICH   I know.

LIDYA PETROVNA   Aleksander Ivanovich, tell me, is this really you?

ALEKSANDER IVANOVICH   I don't understand, Lidya Petrovna.

LIDYA PETROVNA   I cannot be mistaken. I cannot. (*Lowers her voice.*) I even doubt my own children, you know? Now even they confuse me and trouble my heart. But I see that you haven't changed. I know my feelings….

ALEKSANDER IVANOVICH   Lidya Petrovna!

LIDYA PETROVNA   Wait! I know how I feel when I see you and it hasn't changed. Do you understand?

ALEKSANDER IVANOVICH (*kindly*)   No.

LIDYA PETROVNA   I feel the same as I did before. Do you understand? No. No. But where's the proof? How can I be sure that this is really you? This is very important, you know. If it is

The Witching Hour

really you, then everything is the way it was and that woman in the field tricked me. Ah, Aleksander Ivanovich!

ALEKSANDER IVANOVICH You speak so poetically, Lidya Petrovna, I don't understand, but I like to listen to you. I worry about you, you've changed since the potatoes. I give you my word that they won't send you to the state farm again. Let them send younger people. Lidya Petrovna, I have a confession to make, too....

LIDYA PETROVNA About what?

ALEKSANDER IVANOVICH You've just expressed yourself so freely. It's as if it were not me in front of you, but a filing cabinet.

LIDYA PETROVNA No!

ALEKSANDER IVANOVICH Yes, Lidya Petrovna. I've been aware of your feelings toward me for more than five years. And all this time you've kept them to yourself. But today, in passing, you speak about how you feel so casually.... And I'm glad that it can be this way....(*Moves closer to Lidya Petrovna.*)

LIDYA PETROVNA (*frozen*) What are you doing?

ALEKSANDER IVANOVICH Don't say anything, Lidya. My Lidya.

LIDYA PETROVNA A clone.

Pause.

A clone is trying to kiss me. A fake, an imitation Aleksander Ivanovich.

ALEKSANDER IVANOVICH I don't understand you.

LIDYA PETROVNA   It doesn't matter. You can't even fire me, because you don't exist, you see?

ALEKSANDER IVANOVICH   What are you talking about?

LIDYA PETROVNA   And that is the horror of it. If you could understand, you would exist.

ALEKSANDER IVANOVICH   It's … it's some kind of romanticizing. Do try and explain yourself, please.

LIDYA PETROVNA   What's the point of explaining anything if you don't exist?

ALEKSANDER IVANOVICH   Ah, really, what is it with all of you? First Olya, then you.

LIDYA PETROVNA   Olya doesn't exist either.

ALEKSANDER IVANOVICH (*suddenly aware*)   Ah … .you, poor thing, how terrible….

LIDYA PETROVNA (*irritated*)   What do you mean, poor thing? Do you think I'm going crazy?

ALEKSANDER IVANOVICH   Yes.

LIDYA PETROVNA   That would be too simple.

ALEKSANDER IVANOVICH   Well, what should I think?

LIDYA PETROVNA   Prove to me that you exist.

ALEKSANDER IVANOVICH: Why should I have to prove that to you?

LIDYA PETROVNA   Because, I love you, you silly man. You and you alone in this whole empty world. Do you see? And yet I suspect that you don't even exist.

ALEKSANDER IVANOVICH (*confused*)   Could it be that love has driven her crazy? That's so … awful….

LIDYA PETROVNA   Can you just think for a moment that I'm not
  mad? Prove to me that you exist, Aleksander Ivanovich! Please!

ALEKSANDER IVANOVICH   But how can I do that? Isn't it
  obvious already?

LIDYA PETROVNA   Appearances alone aren't enough.

ALEKSANDER IVANOVICH   Touch me.

LIDYA PETROVNA   No, no it's much more complex and intricate
  than that. You see, our world is the exact copy of the real world,
  it's just an imitation.

ALEKSANDER IVANOVICH (*confused*)   Why?

LIDYA PETROVNA   It's for me. For me, so I don't get bored.

ALEKSANDER IVANOVICH (*after a pause*)   I do exist!

LIDYA PETROVNA   Prove it!

ALEKSANDER IVANOVICH   Well, first of all, my mother's still
  alive....

LIDYA PETROVNA   No, no, your mother is just an imitation too.
  Prove it yourself!

ALEKSANDER IVANOVICH (*takes a pocket knife and cuts his finger
  after thinking awhile*)   There!

LIDYA PETROVNA   Oh! Blood!

ALEKSANDER IVANOVICH   But of course, Lidya Petrovna....
  I'm like a crazy teenager, trying to prove to you....

LIDYA PETROVNA   Not good enough.

ALEKSANDER IVANOVICH   But if you examine the blood, you'll
  see that it's real.

LIDYA PETROVNA   It just looks real. Conjured up....

ALEKSANDER IVANOVICH   In the next department, Kurnosova is pregnant. Does she have an imitation in her belly too?

LIDYA PETROVNA   Don't be vulgar….

ALEKSANDER IVANOVICH   Just answer me, please!

LIDYA PETROVNA   You still don't understand what I mean. Everyone's an imitation, except me.

ALEKSANDER IVANOVICH   Except you?

LIDYA PETROVNA   Except me.

ALEKSANDER IVANOVICH   Shall we take a vacation? A trip to the Black Sea?

LIDYA PETROVNA   What for? The Black Sea is a lie. Besides, it's too cold to swim now.

ALEKSANDER IVANOVICH   What happened, anyway?

LIDYA PETROVNA   What do you mean?

ALEKSANDER IVANOVICH   If we're not here, where did we all go?

LIDYA PETROVNA   You wouldn't understand.

ALEKSANDER IVANOVICH   Try to explain.

LIDYA PETROVNA   The surface layer of the earth with everybody on it slid off into the ocean. I was the only one left … except for someone who looks like a woman but is the Evil of the World. She can't survive without me, so she created you for me not to get bored. She said that you would be exactly like the real people I used to know….

ALEKSANDER IVANOVICH   Lidya Petrovna, you should be ashamed of yourself!

The Witching Hour

LIDYA PETROVNA   Why?

ALEKSANDER IVANOVICH   You believe some crazy woman, but not your ... your colleagues.

LIDYA PETROVNA   Aleksander Ivanovich, I brought this upon everybody.

ALEKSANDER IVANOVICH   Really? And how did you do that?

LIDYA PETROVNA   It was this way: if I caught the woman who is the Evil of the World, there would be heaven on earth—well, you know, everyone would be happy, no wars, everyone would have everything and so on.... But if I tried to catch the woman and didn't succeed, everyone would die.

ALEKSANDER IVANOVICH   And you....

LIDYA PETROVNA   I couldn't catch her.

ALEKSANDER IVANOVICH   But how could you have....Who gave you the authority?... to act irresponsibly, and without training.... Do you realize what you've done? Trying to catch a woman without knowing what might come of it?

LIDYA PETROVNA   So, you don't exist, then?

Pause.

ALEKSANDER IVANOVICH   You've got me all confused. (*Worried.*) Are you sure all of this actually happened? That it wasn't a dream, a delusion?

LIDYA PETROVNA   Yes.

ALEKSANDER IVANOVICH   Look at me. Closely. Do I seem strange?

LIDYA PETROVNA   You are the same.

ALEKSANDER IVANOVICH   Look closer. Do you notice anything different?

LIDYA PETROVNA   Why is it so easy for you to believe me?

ALEKSANDER IVANOVICH   Really. (*Astounded.*) Really.

Look at each other.

Because I'm fond of you.

LIDYA PETROVNA   No. It's because you don't exist. You believe me because clones don't care. Prove that you exist.

ALEKSANDER IVANOVICH   But I do care. Let's call on our colleagues.

LIDYA PETROVNA   Who don't exist.

ALEKSANDER IVANOVICH   Well … let's call on their replicas, then.

Elena Maximovna rushes in.

ELENA MAXIMOVNA   Excuse me, my dear comrades, but this is too much even for my patience!

ALEKSANDER IVANOVICH Calm down, former Elena Maximovna!

ELENA MAXIMOVNA   I will not!

ALEKSANDER IVANOVICH (*with dismay*)   The clone is a carbon copy of the original.

LIDYA PETROVNA   There's nothing to laugh about!

ELENA MAXIMOVNA   This doesn't surprise me at all!

ALEKSANDER IVANOVICH   Who asked you?

The Witching Hour

ELENA MAXIMOVNA   Asked me what?

ALEKSANDER IVANOVICH   Anything. Vile creature. Now that we know you don't exist, I can tell you the honest truth: you're a stupid, spiteful pitiful excuse for a woman and you smoke too much!

ELENA MAXIMOVNA   And what will you say when you realize that I do indeed exist?

ALEKSANDER IVANOVICH   Lidya, what does she mean?

LIDYA PETROVNA   Elena Maximovna, dear, prove that you exist.

Aleksander Ivanovich steps away and makes a phone call.

You've always been a respectable, reasonable, capable woman. You've always been on top of things.

ELENA MAXIMOVNA   I exist.

LIDYA PETROVNA   That's all you have to say?

ELENA MAXIMOVNA   It's good enough for me. Let's see what you'll have to say at the meeting….

LIDYA PETROVNA   There won't be a meeting….

ELENA MAXIMOVNA   The meeting is this Wednesday, my dear, at three thirty! Attendance is mandatory!

Olya and Gena come in.

And I suppose they don't exist either?

LIDYA PETROVNA   Aleksander Ivanovich, please, don't turn this into a joke. You've just called an ambulance. I saw you do it! You still think I've gone mad…. I'm not going to the hospital, I'm

183

not. I'm staying right here. I'll live the way I've always lived. It was a mistake to think I can dream of happiness for the world—look what's happened! I've destroyed everyone!...

Everyone is silent.

And you, Olen'ka, you were so young and sweet and spoiled, but I didn't despise you for being young, really, I didn't. I liked you for it. And Gena loved you, Olya, believe me....

OLYA   Lidya Petrovna, has something happened?

ELENA MAXIMOVNA   We don't exist.

OLYA   What on earth do you mean? In what way?

ELENA MAXIMOVNA   In the literal way!

OLYA   Ah, that's so interesting! Gena, we don't exist!

ELENA MAXIMOVNA   Don't you understand? She's insulting us.

LIDYA PETROVNA   No, I'm not insulting you. I'm not. I'd rather you think me sick and crazy, than believe I've insulted you. Please, believe me, my dear comrades ... clones.

ELENA MAXIMOVNA   Did you hear that?!

GENA   Lidya Petrovna, don't worry. You'll get better, I'll come visit you. I'll buy you apples. You like apples. What can I say. Do you hear me? Do you understand?

LIDYA PETROVNA   All right, then. There's still time before the ambulance gets here. Can anyone prove their existence to me? If you can do that—if anyone can do that—I'll be cured without any hospital.

GENA   Can I try?

The Witching Hour

LIDYA PETROVNA   Of course, Gena.

GENA   Well, I've been here for two years, Lidya Petrovna. I came right after graduating college. I like this collective, I like our group. I've found a second family here with you all, even Elena Maximovna. I don't want you to be sick.

ELENA MAXIMOVNA   Oh, come on, nobody wants her to be sick!

GENA   That's just it. If we don't exist, but some sort of imitations have been created in our place ... do I understand you correctly?

LIDYA PETROVNA   That's right. Our world is the exact copy of the real world which has perished.

GENA   ... Then these imitations, they cannot ... cannot reach beyond themselves....

LIDYA PETROVNA   In what sense?

GENA   These imitations are programmed to replicate us in every detail, right?

LIDYA PETROVNA   Yes, Gena, yes! Careful now! Don't let this thought get away! Genochka!

GENA (*with a bright smile*)   It won't get away, Lidya Petrovna, you have known me for two years. Right?

LIDYA PETROVNA   Right.

GENA   And I'm a decent young man. Right?

LIDYA PETROVNA   Without a doubt.

GENA   Six month ago your wallet went missing. Do you remember?

LIDYA PETROVNA   Yes.

GENA   I stole that wallet.

Pause.

LIDYA PETROVNA   I don't understand.

GENA   Lidya Petrovna, nothing in the world would make me reveal this. Even if my mother's life were at stake. Lidya Petrovna, the one who created these copies, imitations, would have made me the same way, you understand? My imitation would never tell you this, he would be ashamed, ashamed in keeping with his personality. Only the real me could reach beyond myself.

Pause.

LIDYA PETROVNA   The wallet?

GENA   The wallet.

LIDYA PETROVNA   You?

GENA   Me.

ELENA MAXIMOVNA   But why?

LIDYA PETROVNA   Gena, Gena, Gena. Forgive me, Gena. Dear, Gena, dear. Forgive me. But this is not proof.

Everyone moves in protest.

GENA   It is proof, Lidya Petrovna, because now I won't be able to live. Neither as an imitation, nor as a real Gena Eskin. I ruined myself with this confession. (*Tries to leave.*)

LIDYA PETROVNA   Wait! If … if you're an imitation, then you shouldn't care.

GENA   But I do care.

LIDYA PETROVNA   To hell with the wallet. Besides, it's the real Gena who did that, not you. You're not responsible for his actions, Gena.

The Witching Hour

GENA   I am responsible. I was made to be like him….

Pause.

LIDYA PETROVNA   You're a stubborn man, I always knew that.

GENA   All right, all right, I'll stay for a while. It's hard for me to leave you all.

OLYA   This is terrible.

GENA   Stay away from me, Olya. I'll rob you. Now I want to steal even more, a feast of crime before the end.

OLYA   Go on, steal, do. I have three rubles.

GENA   (*painfully*)   And she doesn't exist? Our Olen'ka doesn't exist?

LIDYA PETROVNA   If she can prove it, then she does.

OLYA   Well, at least, this is more fun than being stuck behind a desk. I'll prove I exist. I do, because … first of all … but promise not to laugh! It may seem silly, but don't laugh. Not yet!

GENA   We won't laugh!

OLYA   Gena confessed that he was a thief. He considers this the most convincing proof of being human.

GENA   I don't think that….

OLYA   Quiet. If the issue is before us, we have to deal with it. So, I am alive!

ELENA MAXIMOVNA   There she goes again….

OLYA   Elena Maximovna, you don't like this question for some reason. But I like it. It's as if I knew yesterday that this would happen today. I am alive. And I'm bored. (*To Lidya Petrovna.*) You said these imitations are made so convincingly, they replicate the very essence of a real human being?

LIDYA PETROVNA   Yes.

OLYA   Well, all right. I'm bored with my life. I feel good knowing that Gena is in love with me. I like people (*a gesture towards Lidya Petrovna*) and I dislike people (*a gesture towards Elena Maximovna*). But I know that I haven't started living yet. I don't have as good of an argument as Gena's, and I haven't achieved much, but I'm deeply sure that I am alive, that I'm real, and that I'm not a copy....

GENA   Yes, I'm sure of that as well, Olen'ka.

OLYA   Tell me, are these imitations able to reproduce themselves?

LIDYA PETROVNA   Of course they are.

OLYA   Then I don't know how else to convince you. (*With reproach.*) Lidya Petrovna, can you really think of us this way? Lidya Petrovna?

LIDYA PETROVNA   Elena Maximovna, now you're the only one without an opinion. Don't argue. The issue is pressing. At least try to prove it.

ELENA MAXIMOVNA   No way!

LIDYA PETROVNA   Elena Maximovna!

ALEKSANDER IVANOVICH   Wait, Lidya Petrovna, Gena actually convinced me.

LIDYA PETROVNA   Did he?

ALEKSANDER IVANOVICH   But of course. A confession like that isn't a joke. Only a human being can do that.

The Witching Hour

GENA   Thank you.

ALEKSANDER IVANOVICH   If we follow the principle of shameful confessions, if that's the way to prove anything, then I....

LIDYA PETROVNA   Don't. That's not proof. Can't you see?

ALEKSANDER IVANOVICH   Why not? Don't you care what a clone tells you?

LIDYA PETROVNA   I don't.

ALEKSANDER IVANOVICH   Then admit that we exist—all of us.

LIDYA PETROVNA   No.

ALEKSANDER IVANOVICH   Listen then. I'm a monster.

ELENA MAXIMOVNA   She's the one who doesn't exist.

Pause

LIDYA PETROVNA   What?

ELENA MAXIMOVNA   Yes, let her prove that *she* exists.

LIDYA PETROVNA   Why a monster?

ALEKSANDER IVANOVICH   Never mind. We're waiting. Prove that *you* exist.

LIDYA PETROVNA   Me? Why? I *know* that I exist.

ELENA MAXIMOVNA   Oh, yes, everyone knows.

LIDYA PETROVNA   But I really know.

ELENA MAXIMOVNA   So does everyone else.

LIDYA PETROVNA   The point is this idea came to me.

ELENA MAXIMOVNA   A real human being wouldn't get such ideas.

LIDYA PETROVNA   What?

ELENA MAXIMOVNA   You don't exist. You've been replaced by an imitation, my friend.

LIDYA PETROVNA   Me?

ELENA MAXIMOVNA   You.

LIDYA PETROVNA (*mumbles*)   Only you will rot, like potatoes in dirt, and everyone else will blossom, like angels in heaven, like apple trees, like God's flowers....

ELENA MAXIMOVNA   Yea, that's right. You've died....

LIDYA PETROVNA   Oh, Auntie! It's stopped aching. My heart. It doesn't hurt anymore. But you … are you the angels of heaven?

ELENA MAXIMOVNA   Yes, we are.

LIDYA PETROVNA   God's flowers?

ELENA MAXIMOVNA   Are you jealous?

LIDYA PETROVNA   No, but why don't I see it?

ELENA MAXIMOVNA   Because you can't. You're dead.

LIDYA PETROVNA   Really? Really? Is it true? You exist? All of you? That means I didn't kill you?

ELENA MAXIMOVNA   No, you didn't. You killed *yourself*. And we're all here, we're all alive.

LIDYA PETROVNA   My God … my God, so everyone lives? The whole world!

ELENA MAXIMOVNA   But you don't! You lie in the ground and rot!

LIDYA PETROVNA   Flowers, angels. Happiness!

The piercing wail of an ambulance siren is heard.

Only my heart, my heart has stopped. I'm alone, but I lie in the deep, moist earth, and the world blooms, happy, joyous, and alive! Farewell! Live long and prosper, love, give birth, work and rest! Farewell!

Lidya Petrovna runs out. Silence. A phone rings.

ELENA MAXIMOVNA (*into the phone*)   Engineers' office. She … she just left. What? Speak clearly, please. Promised what? What stockings? What Auntie? Oh!

(Grabs her chest. Busy signal on the phone.)

CURTAIN

Translated from the Russian
*by **Anna Gordeichuk** and **Nadya L. Peterson***

Afterword

Karin Sarsenov

In the course of Nina Sadur's career, the place of the writer in Russian culture changed dramatically. The Socialist Realist "engineers of the human soul" reflecting "the consciousness of the people" exchanged their formulaic narratives of a glorious Communist future for more pedestrian offerings. Literature with high artistic ambitions became marginalized by popular fiction, TV serials, and social media.

As a young writer, Sadur struggled to gain recognition from the Soviet literary establishment and was categorically rejected because of the "unseemly" originality and the experimental reach of the work she produced. Except for a brief period during perestroika, when her formerly unpublishable plays attracted large audiences in Moscow theaters, Sadur has remained a writer at the margins in all senses: as a provincial in Moscow, as a woman in a male-dominated cultural environment, as an outsider among literary groupings during the period of "stagnation," and, most importantly, as a writer whose concerns lie on the periphery of social community and empirical reality. Even her occasional forays into popular culture as a scriptwriter show her predilection for the liminal. In 2004 Sadur appeared in the credits of *The Female Taxi Driver* (*Taksistka*), a prime-time TV serial in twelve parts, whose heroine roams the Moscow streets after her profession as an organizer of political celebrations at a house of pioneers evaporates.

Due to Sadur's emphatic incompatibility with the aesthetics of Socialist Realism, the bulk of her work was published only in the 1990s. At that time she was drawn, unwillingly, into the battle between the "realists" and the "postmodernists," neither of whom impressed her. She belonged to a sizable group of authors uninterested in theoretical and analytical considerations, who avoided labels, theses, and manifestos. Mark Lipovetsky (2000) has proposed the term "neo-sentimentalism" to describe this "manhole" between realism and postmodernism. Its representatives (Lipovetsky mentions Timur Kibirov, Evgenii Kharitonov, Liudmila Ulitskaia, Marina Palei, and Galina Scherbakova) demonstrate the possibility of a literature that questions the capacity of language to capture a fragmented social reality, yet avoids the intertextual playfulness of postmodernism. The "sentimentalism" of this literature is expressed by a heightened attention to corporeality, whereby suspicion towards the world of reason generates a confidence in the body and its sensations as bearers of meaning. Sadur's use of corporeality is rather distinctive, insofar as the physical atrocities to which she subjects her characters are part of an intertextual play with incantations and spells from Russian folklore. Nevertheless, her professed distrust of rationality and her belief in the spiritual aspect of bodily functions connect her with the neo-sentimentalists as described by Lipovetsky.

Born Nina Nikolaevna Kolesnikova in 1950 in Novosibirsk, and raised by her mother, Sadur never felt socially vulnerable, for the reputation of her father, Nikolai Perevalov—a renowned poet and a hero of World War II—shielded the family.[1] After his separation from her mother, his poet's salary enabled Perevalov to pay generous alimony to his ex-wife, but his bohemian mode of existence prevented him from participating in family life. Sadur

---

[1] All biographical information in this article comes from a recorded interview with Nina Sadur on November 24, 2004.

drew closer to him in her teens and adopted the same lifestyle for herself. Instead of going to university after graduating from high school, she spent time with her circle of poet-friends: Ivan Chigov, Aleksander Denisenko, Anatolii Makovskii, and Ivan Zelenin. She subsequently became a member of Il'ia Foniakov's "lito" (literary association), which facilitated her access to print, since the main editor of the journal *Sibirskie ogni* belonged to the group. Sadur made her literary debut on its pages in 1974 with the unpretentious story "We Go to Work with a Song in our Hearts" ("Na rabotu s pesnei my idem"), and followed up this publication with the novella *This Is My Window* (*Eto moe okno*) in 1977. Both works describe a young girl's initiation into adult life.

Novosibirsk appears frequently in her oeuvre: as the provincial town to which it is impossible to return (as in "A New Friendship" ["Novoe znakomstvo"] and "Something Will Reveal Itself" ["Chto-to otkroetsia"]) or as the site of a warm, safe childhood in a snowy landscape (as in *The Garden* [*Sad*] and *Permafrost* [*Vechnaia merzlota*]). The experience of a fatherless upbringing is also represented, as seen for example in Larisa's soliloquy in "A New Friendship":

> It was only the Rogachevs who used to say that our Mom was a useless hussy and we were God only knows what: who were our Dads? Where were they? What would become of us? They were all shook up about that—what would become of us. And the reason they said that was because they themselves did not have anything besides money, but our Mom had her beauty and a dress with a little black bow and lovers and she also had us! (34)

However, there are also darker images to be found in the stories of that period. In *This is My Window*, a passage with striking autobiographical parallels describes the traumatic experience of having a father who, while officially a hero, is in fact an abusive alcoholic:

> A narrow room where they lived, the three of them, a late evening, Father's drunken laughter, Mom, running around the room with tousled hair and matches.... Father lighted them and threw them at Mom's hair.... Then Tania had to learn how to lie.

> She was ashamed of lying, but she had to, for some reason. She understood that heroes were not like Dad. But Dad was as much a hero as you could be—he had a medal "For Bravery"? (59)

At the age of twenty-one Nina married a fellow writer, Oleg Gareevich Sadur, an ethnic Tatar who, after their divorce, became the model for the demonic Dyrdybai in the novel *Sad*. Sadur herself claims to be Russian, dismissing suggestions that she is Tatar or Jewish. She traces her genealogy to Tambov on one side and to the Old Believers on the other. Her work teems with colorful pictures of non-Russians, pictures that emphasize their otherness and evoke associations with earlier Orientalist portraits by Russian Romanticists or the philosophical racism expressed by Vladimir Solov'ev and his followers. When asked to comment on this issue in an interview, Sadur made a strong statement of her rights as an artist:

> I am an artist, I allow for differences among people. [My protagonist] is totally different, he has different habits, different manners. It's a whole palette of colors. Of course I make use of it. It's a whole world, inconceivable.... But I am interested in everything about him, everything about what he's like. Why do I have to pussyfoot around it if he has some traits I don't like? Pussyfooting is really the hypocritical side of racism.[2]

In 1973 Sadur gave birth to a daughter, Ekaterina. The experience of childbirth is a recurring, yet contradictory, motif in Sadur's work. Traditionally, the bodily processes of conception, pregnancy, and delivery have served as the emblems of womanhood while simultaneously being tabooed and, therefore, narratively underrepresented in Western culture. In Sadur's work they are revealed in all their complexity, with a sharp focus on their emotional and spiritual aspects.

The contradictory experience of witnessing the miracle of a budding life and of harboring an alien body within one's own

---

[2] Recorded interview on November 24, 2004.

becomes a matter of escalating intensity in her work. In *This Is My Window*, the latter feeling dominates:

> The thing was that she didn't know whether she wanted a baby. For some reason everybody thought that you had to want one. How could you possibly want somebody *unknown*? For everybody, even for Lenka, she … ceased to exist as simply Tania; for them she became a vessel, a cover for somebody, whose face nobody yet knew." (Sadur's emphasis) (66)

In the novella Tania consistently chooses to associate with strange, randomly chosen people over those who mean the most to her. Consequently, her period of pregnancy is related as a story of friendship with *another child*, with whom she gets acquainted by chance. When the baby appears, it has a "strange, vaguely familiar face" and is immediately abandoned by Tania to be brought up by its grandmother. One discerns the same kind of estrangement in the novel *Sad*, in which the pregnant body, through displacement, becomes an expanding bubble stuck to a radiator.

The conflicting desires spurred by pregnancy—to be loved for one's own sake and to care for the unborn—structure the plot of the 1987 play *While Still Alive* (*Poka zhivye*). A young couple visits their old relatives in the countryside, inviting them to come to their apartment in the city as volunteer nannies for the expected baby. The young couple's entrance into the realm of the superstition, poverty, and illiteracy of the village crudely jolts them out of their well-arranged life and modes of thought. The young wife's confrontation with one of the village women, who is skilled in magic, leads her to acknowledge a strong desire for passionate love and a readiness to sacrifice her child to that end. As in many stories by Sadur, the sorceress proves to be the narrative's most authoritative protagonist, whose concern is primarily for the unborn child:

> You're carrying him now, you have to walk around quietly. The blood in you is quiet, nourishing, nutritious for your child. But if I stir you all up? Set you on fire? What'll happen then? (21)

A similar concern is attributed to the half-witted Tikusia in the play *Loving People* (*Liubovnye liudi*, 1979). Tikusia's mental disorder

Afterword — Karin Sarsenov

is manifested in her nocturnal conversations with a three-year-old child burning in napalm whose image she sees in a magazine. Tikusia carries the illusory child in her arms and imagines a reversed birth:

> Cuddle up against me now and don't breathe, dissolve in me and I'll never give birth to you, I'll hide you from everybody and you'll be safe. (166)

The son of Tikusia's neighbor serves as yet another surrogate child for the protagonist. Tikusia's heightened sensitivity gives her intuitive knowledge about the transgression of the boy's father, who forced his wife to abandon the child at birth. The boy's dysfunctional upbringing has resulted in a life in and out of prison, and Tikusia's desire to bring him back to the womb seems suddenly rational. If in *While Still Alive* the woman's hesitation about abandoning her body and her life to something unknown presents a challenge to motherhood, in *Loving People* the ambivalence of fatherhood constitutes the main threat to the child. In both plays, the destructive and procreative forces are monitored by the figure of the madwoman/witch/healer.

However, despite the clearly declared feelings of alienation in connection with childbirth, the mystic power of life-giving motherhood is present to an equal extent in Sadur's work. In *Everything Is Forbidden* (*Zapreshcheno—vse*) the untouchable sacredness of a mother with her newborn baby in a pram is presented against the background of the debauchery taking place in the basement of her house. Here, the voice of the newborn child transforms into a shield, capable of protecting the vulnerable, unmarried mother.

In 1978 Sadur enrolled in Viktor Rozov's theater seminar at the Gor'kii Literary Institute in Moscow. After a brief period in the Institute's dormitory, she moved with her family to a dacha in Vostriakovo, within commuting distance of Moscow. This was a productive time in her life: the plays *The Witching Hour* (*Chudnaia baba*, 1983), *Dawn Will Rise* (*Zaria vzoidet*, 1982), *Loving People* (*Liubovnye liudi*, 1979), and *The Devil in Love* (*Vliublennyi d'iavol*, 1983) were written here. Vostriakovo, a provincial, isolated site, figures in such novellas as *The Girl at Night* (*Devochka noch'iu*, 1981) and *South* (*Iug*, 1992). None of these plays was published before perestroika, however; editors judged their metaphysical bent and existential despair unsuitable for Soviet readers.

Sadur's next "home," a communal apartment close to Patriarch's Ponds in central Moscow, also spurred her creativity. Her ordinary neighbors across the hall were transformed in Sadur's prose into grotesque monsters or pitiful victims, such as Mar'ia Ivanovna, the prey of the Blue Hand in the story named for that figure, the promiscuous Farida in *The Diamond Valley* (*Almaznaia dolina*), or the six-fingered Polugarmon' (Semi-Accordion) in *The Wondrous Signs of Salvation* (*Chudesnye znaki spasen'ia*). Sadur's work from this period contributed to a large corpus of "communal art" in Soviet/Russian culture—artistic interpretations based on the provisional Soviet housing experiment that became a permanent tool of surveillance by the state. Whereas films such as *The Pokrov Gates* (*Pokrovskie vorota*, 1982), *Everything Will Be Fine* (*Vse budet khorosho*, 1995), and *Life is Full of Fun* (*Zhizn' zabavami polna*, 2003) emphasize the atmosphere of mutual support and solidarity in these domiciles, and songs such as Bulat Okudzhava's "The Black Cat" ("Chernyi kot") and Diuna's "The Communal Apartment" ("Kommunal'naia kvartira") center on their political aspects, Sadur's primary concern is the violation of private space constantly occurring within the permeable walls of the apartment.

Sadur graduated from the Literary Institute in 1983, embarking on the path of self-supporting mother and nonconformist author. Her work as a cleaning lady in the Pushkin Theater is reflected in such stories as "Frozen" ("Zamerzli") and "The Wormy Son" (Chervivyi synok) from the cycle *Discerning* (*Pronikshie*).

Perestroika finally put an end to Sadur's literary invisibility. In 1987, the student theater at Moscow State University staged *The Witching Hour*, and established theaters soon followed suit, including Lenkom (Lenin's Komsomol Theater) and the Ermolov Theater. In 1989 she published her first collection of plays, *Chudnaia baba*, which contains the bulk of the texts written during her years in obscurity. Two plays in this volume, *The Witching Hour* (*Chudnaia baba*) and *Move It!* (*Ekhai!*), come from this first collection.

By late perestroika Sadur had managed to exchange her four rooms in the *kommunalka* for an apartment of her own on Nikitskii Boulevard, in the "house of the polar explorers," close to Nikolai Andreev's Gogol monument and next to the mansion where Gogol burned the second part of *Dead Souls*. Like the more mundane localities of her earlier years, these historical sites inevitably made their ways into her works. Gogol's statue figures as a silent witness and interpreter of the lives of the homeless in *The Garden* (*Sad*, 1997) and as an unfortunate object of children's mockery in *South* (*Iug*). Gogol is also a cherished source for her dramatic adaptations (Gogol's story "Vii" translates into Sadur's play *Pannochka*; *Dead Souls* is staged as *Brat Chichikov [Brother Chichikov]*). Built in 1935 to accommodate the heroes of the Soviet polar expeditions, Nikitskii Boulevard no. 9 witnessed the atrocities of Stalinist persecutions, and in *Permafrost* (2002) Sadur vividly transforms it into a basement populated by starving, dislocated elderly people.

In "An Old Man and a Hat" ("Starik i shapka") written in 1993, the history of the house generates a meditation on Russia's contemporary history:

> Time was, they demanded cheerful, faithful energy from all of our people to last for a thousand years with nothing in return. And the people happily gave what was required, and the polar explorer departed dressed in boots, and his fragile feet were squeezed by the tender cold of the polar region, and the Kremlin stars roiled in steamy ruby-colored blood, and arrogant fireworks thundered in the green sky, and the dead man roared with laughter in the Mausoleum, and the happiness of the downtrodden sparkled. (381)

The attempt to capture the Soviet experience continues in *The Garden*, in which the Kremlin appears in images associated with the Snow Queen's enchanted kingdom in Hans Christian Andersen's tale of that figure.

During the nineties, Sadur turned from drama to fiction: her first prose collection, *Witch's Tears* (*Ved'miny slezki*) was published by Glagol in 1994, and in 1997 the volume *The Garden* (*Sad*) appeared in Vologda, sponsored by the businessman German Titov. The limited circulation and admittedly poor typography of the latter collection presumably explain why most novels and stories from the collection have been republished in *Wondrous Signs* (*Chudeznye znaki*, 2000) or *Angry Girls* (*Zlye devushki*, 2003). Sadur's prose of the nineties is distinguished by an increasing interest in linguistic experimentation amidst her continued engagement with the folkloric and supernatural. If the stories in *Discerning* (published in 1990) were enigmatic due to their hints at an unknown reality (though they were narrated in a simple, straightforward manner), the novels *The Garden* and *The German* (*Nemets*) and the collection *The Immortals* (*Bessmertniki*) approach this reality by means of deliberately obscure narrative strategies, bringing Sadur's work of the period closer to the aesthetics of early modernism.

Sadur's most recent original book-length publication, *Permafrost* (*Vechnaia merzlota*, 2004) contains, in addition to several plays and stories, the novella that lends its title to the volume. According to Sadur, this novella is the book's sole *raison d'être*: the other texts — including three stories previously published in erotic magazines — were added to make for a book-length manuscript. Two plays appearing in this volume, *Red Paradise* and *Pechorin: In Memoriam* (*Zovite Pechorinym*), are translations of texts from *Permafrost*.

In 1999 Sadur published a new collection of plays, *The Fainting Spell* (*Obmorok*), also sponsored by Titov, and in 2001 one of them, *Brother Chichikov* (*Brat Chichikov*, an adaptation of Gogol's *Dead Souls*) had great success in a staging by Mark Zakharov at Lenkom. That year the Pushkin Theater, where Sadur had formerly worked as a cleaning lady, performed *Pechorin: In Memoriam*, based on Lermontov's novel *A Hero of Our Time*.

For many women authors, writing scripts for light Russian TV entertainment has been a welcome source of income, and Sadur has benefited from this boom. During the 2000s, she regularly authored scripts for high-profile TV serials such as *Rostov-papa*, *Taksistka*, and *Ligovka*. In 2010, after a break in her literary pursuits, she published several stories and plays in Siberian thick journals and online. Here, she returns to her investigation of the minds of urban outcasts in a post-Soviet society. Sadur's new plays, *The Doctor of the Garden* (*Doktor Sada*, 2011) and *The Pilot* (*Liotchik*, 2009), feature characters and situations found in the novella *Permafrost* and in her story "The

List of References

Antologiia sovremennogo rasskaza, ed. Aleksandr Mikhailov. Moscow: Ast, Olimp, 2002.

Lipovetsky, Mark. "Literature on the Margins: Russian Fiction in the Nineties." *Studies in Twentieth-Century Literature* 24, no.1 (Winter, 2000): 139-68.

Sadur, Nina. "Na rabotu s pesnei my idem." *Sibirskie ogni* 7 (1974): 190-92

------."Eto moe okno." *Sibirskie ogni* 7 (1977): 53-88.

------. "Novoe znakomstvo: p'esa v dvukh deistviiakh." *Teatr* 4 (1986): 25-48.

------. "Poka zhivye: p'esa v 7 kartinkakh." In *VAAP-inform.* Moscow, 1987.

------. *Pronikshie. Ne pomiashchaia zla,* ed. L.L. Vaneeva. Moscow, 1990. 217-48.

------. "Iug." *Znamia* 10 (1992): 19-40.

------. "Chto-to otkroetsia." *Vidimost' nas,* ed. O. Dark. Moscow, 1991. 44-55.

------. "Sad, Nemets, Almaznaia dolina, Bessmertniki." In *Sad.* Vologda: Poligrafist, 87-177.

------. "O realizme prozrachnogo." *Zolotoi vek* 10 (1997): 82-84.

------. "Liubovnye liudi," "Chudnaia baba," "Zaria vzoidet," and "Vliublennyi d'iavol." In *Obmorok. Kniga p'es.* Vologda: Poligrafist, 1999.

------. "Chudesnye znaki spasen'ia," "Devochka nochiu," "Zapreshcheno— vse," and "Starik i shapka." In *Chudeznye znaki. Romany, povest', rasskazy.* Moskva: Vagrius, 2000.

------. "Vechnaia merzlota." In *Vechnaia merzlota.* Moscow: Zebra E; Ehksmo-Press, 2004.

------. "Mal'chik v chernom plashche." *Sibirskie ogni* 1 (2011)a.

------. "Letchik." *Ural* 1 (2011).

Sarsenov, Karin. *Passion Embracing Death. A Reading of Nina Sadur's Novel The Garden.* Lund: Lund Slavonic Monographs, 2001.

Dead Hour" (both from the collection *Permafrost*). In January of 2013 Sadur finished a new play, *Falalei*, loosely based on Antonii Pogorel'skii's novella *Lafertovskaia Makovnitsa* (*The Lafertovo Poppy-Seed Cake Seller*). In the play, Sadur returns to "hovering" between straightforward realistic representation of events and the folklore-based fantasy characteristic of her work of the 1980s.

Sadur's work is situated in the twilight zone between a readily recognizable empirical reality and "the other side" — an indefinable reality that Sadur conjures up with her densely metaphorical and often poetic language. Her literary space is overtly gynocentric: the fictional world construes women's traditionally downplayed concerns as narratively and existentially central and crucial. Exploration of the metaphysical periphery — *okraina* — has become the hallmark of Sadur's writing. Although critics sometimes situate her among the postmodernists, Sadur herself characterizes her prose as "realism of the illusory," linking her role as a writer to that of a shaman whose sensibility enables him to approach other worlds that are enriching yet dangerous.

With the exception of Liudmila Petrushevskaia's dramatic output, Soviet/Russian drama of the 1980s and 1990s has been generally ignored by the Western literary establishment. Nina Sadur, as a playwright, has earned one of the most prominent places in the Russian literary pantheon of the period. The plays included in this volume offer some of Sadur's most influential works for the theater to an English-speaking audience for the first time.